Leading With the Brain in Mind

Leading With the Brain in Mind

101 Brain-Compatible Practices for Leaders

Michael H. Dickmann
Nancy Stanford-Blair
Anthea Rosati-Bojar

CORWIN PRESS
A Sage Publications Company
Thousand Oaks, California

For information:

Corwin Press
A Sage Publications Company
2455 Teller Road
Thousand Oaks, California 91320
www.corwinpress.com

Sage Publications Ltd.
6 Bonhill Street
London EC2A 4PU
United Kingdom

Sage Publications India Pvt. Ltd.
B-42, Panchsheel Enclave
Post Box 4109
New Delhi 110 017 India

Printed in the United States of America

Library of Congress Cataloging-in-Publication Data

Dickmann, Michael Haley.
Leading with the brain in mind : 101 brain-compatible practices for leaders / by Michael H. Dickmann, Nancy Standford-Blair, Anthea Rosati-Bojar.
    p. cm.
Includes bibliographical references and index.
ISBN 0-7619-3948-2 (hc) — ISBN 0-7619-3949-0 (pb))
    1. Leadership. 2. Intellect. I. Stanford-Blair, Nancy.
II. Rosati-Bojar, Anthea. III. Title.
HM1261.D533 2004
303.3'4—dc222

                                          2003016455

This book is printed on acid-free paper.

03   04   05   06   07   10   9   8   7   6   5   4   3   2   1

Acquisitions Editor:	Robert D. Clouse
Editorial Assistant:	Jingle Vea
Production Editor:	Julia Parnell
Copy Editor:	Ruth Saavedra
Typesetter:	C&M Digitals (P) Ltd.
Proofreader:	Sally M. Scott
Indexer:	Kay Dushek
Cover Designer:	Michael Dubowe
Graphic Designer:	Lisa Miller

Contents

Preface:
A Leadership Leap

*A lot of people experience the world with the same incredulity as when
a magician suddenly pulls a rabbit out of a hat . . .*

—Jostein Gaarder (1996, p.14)

In explaining the work of philosophers to the character of a 14-year-old
schoolgirl in *Sophie's World*, Gaarder (1996) uses the metaphor of a white
rabbit pulled from a magician's hat. For various reasons, he observes, the
inclination to question the nature of the world becomes diminished in many
people. As they become caught up in everyday affairs, their fundamental
questions about the world get pushed into the background. They "crawl deep
into the rabbit's fur," opting for a more comfortable, less inquisitive orientation to the nature of their existence (p. 17). Philosophers, on the other hand,
"climb up the fine hairs of the rabbit's fur in order to stare right into the
magician's eyes" (p.14). It is this pursuit of answers to fundamental questions about the origin, purpose, and destination of the universe, according
to Gaarder, that distinguishes philosophers from the majority of the residents
of the world.

Like philosophers, leaders seek additional perspective by moving in mind
and spirit to the ends of what is familiar and comfortable. They pursue
answers to questions that challenge established perceptions of what, when,
where, why, and how. Leaders, moreover, distinguish themselves beyond the
challenges associated with intellectual exploration. They act on new insight
as it evolves. Leaders do not move to the edge merely to see what they might
see. They step forward, leaping the gap between what is familiar but suspect

to that which is more accurate and productive. In this manner, new frontiers are bridged to meaningful adjustments in the conduct of human affairs.

The intent of a prior work, *Connecting Leadership to the Brain* (Dickmann & Stanford-Blair, 2002), was to move leadership to the ends of the hairs of the rabbit—to help leaders engage breakthrough knowledge about human capacity for learning and achievement. The assumption was that emerging intelligence research and theory favorably informs leaders about how to best influence the achievement of worthy goals. There is more work to be done, however, in helping leaders make the leap from informed perception to compatible practice. Perception of the merits of intelligence-friendly leadership will result in little more than intellectual sound and fury if action does not follow insight.

To that end, *Leading With the Brain in Mind* is a practitioner's book that details practical leadership strategies and practices. It aspires to both encourage and facilitate a leap to a new leadership paradigm—one that is more mindful of the nature and nurture of intelligence in the process of influencing others toward the achievement of goals.

Acknowledgments

The composition of a book is never the work of the authors alone. Accordingly, *Leading With the Brain in Mind* is the product of many influences in the process of its conception, development, and production. The authors are first and foremost indebted to the scientific community that has collectively engineered spectacular breakthroughs in knowledge about the nature of human capacity for learning and achievement. It is contemporary revelation about brain-enabled intelligence that makes it possible to tighten leadership alignment to such capacity. Similarly, the evolution of this book is indebted to the growing community of scholars who are exploring informed leadership connections to the nature of human intelligence capacity. The authors appreciate the example, inspiration, and support they receive from all those who labor in the same field of interest about productive leadership influence on human systems. The authors also acknowledge the encouragement and advice received from colleagues and students in the College of Education and the Leadership Center at Cardinal Stritch University. Finally, the publishing staff at Corwin Press has, once again, provided invaluable guidance and support for our scholarship efforts.

The authors also wish to join Corwin Press in gratefully acknowledging the contributions of the following reviewers:

Robert D. Ramsey
Author
Minneapolis, MN

Jeffrey Glanz
Author
Dean, Department
    of Education
Wagner College
Staten Island, NY

David W. Johnson
Co-Director
Cooperative Learning Center
University of Minnesota
Edina, MN

Roland S. Barth
Author, Educator
Alna, ME

Tara Fair
Principal
Central Middle School
2001-2002 Secondary Blue Ribbon School
Edmond, OK

Pat Wolfe
Educational Consultant
Mind Matter, Inc.
Napa, CA

Roger T. Johnson
Co-Director
Cooperative Learning Center
University of Minnesota
Edina, MN

About the Authors

Michael H. Dickmann and **Nancy Stanford-Blair** are professors in the Department of Educational Leadership and the Leadership Center at Cardinal Stritch University in Milwaukee, Wisconsin. **Anthea Rosati-Bojar** is Dean of the College of Education at Cardinal Stritch University. In their university roles, the authors teach, advise, and conduct research in the areas of leadership, learning, and service. They are also consultants to education, business, and service organizations in matters of leadership. learning, and development. They can be contacted at

mhdickmann@stritch.edu

nsblair@aol.com

albojar@stritch.edu

To leaders who seek to be informed so that they might better perform and transform

Introduction: Making the Leap

Reality doesn't change itself. We need to act.

—Wheatley (2002, p. 51)

Moving From Perception to Performance

It is time to lead with the brain in mind. Emerging revelations about the brain are of natural interest to parents, educators, CEOs, and all others in a position to influence the success of others. This is a breakthrough opportunity for everyone on the leadership continuum to better understand the neural roots of human capacity. It is a moment, moreover, for a pragmatic push that moves leaders from informed perception to improved performance. This book aspires to provide such a nudge.

The intent of *Leading With the Brain in Mind*, then, is to help leaders act on new knowledge about how people learn and achieve. This is essential because, if you are a leader, understanding the significance of a challenge or opportunity is prerequisite and important, but not sufficient. Perception of what is important and a dollar or two will buy a cup of coffee. Until you make the leap and act on what is important, you are a looker, not a leader. It is in the performance—the doing—that the leadership difference is made.

A Pragmatic Proposal

Leaders are disposed to act. Whether they are educators, politicians, warriors, activists, or explorers, leaders act on perceptions of what is important. They move from perception to performance. After they "see it" they proceed to do something about it.

This work serves the leadership disposition to perform. Specifically, it proposes to bridge knowledge about the nature of intelligence to practical practices that nurture that capacity toward the achievement of goals. It is a proposal that aspires to be immediately useful in helping leaders move from "seeing" the nature of human capacity to doing something about it. In this effort, *Leading With the Brain in Mind* is aligned to the premises introduced in *Connecting Leadership to the Brain* (Dickmann & Stanford-Blair, 2002). This work complements that earlier project by translating conceptual ideas into specific applications. It is also designed to stand on its own, however, as a contribution to a growing body of literature that examines the leadership relationship to human capacity, including the works of Peter Senge (1990, 1994); Margaret Wheatley (1992, 2002); Howard Gardner (1995, 1997); Elkhonon Goldberg (2001); Michael Fullan (2001, 2003); and Daniel Goleman, Richard Boyatzis, and Anne McKee (2002).

The pragmatic focus of this particular work, then, recognizes that new insight into the nature of human capacity will remain an intellectual epiphany until acted on in a leadership context. The organization of the book also adopts a practical approach to accommodate the needs and interests of diverse readers.

A Practical Approach

A book intended to be of practical use requires a practical approach to content. Accordingly, *Leading With the Brain in Mind* regulates theoretical musings to a minor role in favor of straightforward accounts of what is important to know and do. That is, brain research and theory is translated into practical descriptions of (1) *what* leaders aspire to influence in others and (2) *how* leaders might best influence such capacity.

A second influence on the organization of the book's content is the diversity of prior knowledge readers will bring to this work. Readers should engage the book in whatever fashion best serves their needs. Most will sequentially engage the *what* and *how* of *Leading With the Brain in Mind* as it unfolds in Chapters 1–9. Others will read the last chapter first to reference what leading with the brain in mind might look like in a "capacity-connected" culture. Another approach would be to selectively read chapter sections that address specific dimensions of intelligence and/or aligned leadership strategies and practices. The brief overview of the book's organization and content that follows will assist your decision about how you will engage it.

Part One: Perception

Part One establishes the perspective of the leadership-intelligence connection and forecasts its greater potential. Those who have read *Connecting Leadership to the Brain* (Dickmann & Stanford-Blair, 2002) will find this short section to be an updated summary of concepts put forth in that earlier work. For that reason, readers who are already familiar with this content might fast-forward to Part Two. Those who do engage the opening two chapters of the book will briefly preview

The Connection: leadership as a process of influencing others toward the achievement of goals, a process that is influenced by breakthrough knowledge about the brain in the context of the twenty-first century.

The Connected Leader: an emerging leadership paradigm, one that is mindful of the nature and nurture of human intelligence in influencing organizational culture and achievement.

Part Two: Performance

Part Two employs the power of story to bridge perceptions about the multidimensional nature of intelligence to 15 strategies and 101 aligned practices that nurture those capacities in individuals and groups. This middle six-chapter portion represents the "practical" meat of the book, but reader discretion is appropriate here as well. Readers who are already well informed about the physiological, social, emotional, constructive, reflective, or dispositional dimensions of brain-enabled intelligence from other sources might forego the summary accounts provided in the beginning of specific chapters. Instead, they might elect to cut to the chase and immediately entertain the aligned strategies and practices described in the latter half of each chapter.

Readers who do engage the full content of Chapters 3–8 will rediscover that their brain loves a good story—because it can. Your brain particularly enjoys a story about itself, and of late, it is possible for it to access intriguing revelations from brain research and theory. Accordingly, the middle chapters will appeal to your brain's self-interest in such accounts by presenting short stories describing multiple dimensions of intelligence capacity—what they are and how they work, as well as why they matter and what might be done to exercise them well.

The six stories are purposefully aligned to a cast of fictional characters to engage brain processing of content in a manner that is consistent with its natural approach to constructing knowledge. Connecting fictional names to chapter narratives associates flesh and blood with the bones of technical information. To further enhance this effect, the reader is invited to override the fictional names with names of colleagues who are relevant to his or her leadership context.

Specifically, the six stories address

The *physiological dimension* of intelligence as described through the story of "Brian, The Big Brain"—the story of the biological platform of cells, circuits, and chemicals upon which brain capacity for information processing operates. (Note: This first story is a bit longer because it establishes a base for the following five.)

The *social dimension* of intelligence as described through the story of "Evelyn, The Extrovert"—the story of the capacity for social interaction that the brain expects and depends on to do its job well

The *emotional dimension* of intelligence as described through the story of "Arnold, The Arouser"—the story of the capacity by which the brain is aroused to attention, makes judgments, and is motivated

The *constructive dimension* of intelligence as described through the story of "Pat, The Pattern Maker"—the story of the extraordinary brain capacity for perceiving, organizing, and remembering useful information patterns

The *reflective dimension* of intelligence as described through the story of "Manuel, The Manipulator"—the story of the distinguishing brain capacity for consciously manipulating information to review, analyze, project, rehearse, and create

The *dispositional dimension* of intelligence as described through the story of "Maxine, The Maximizer"—the story of brain capacity for developing and employing mental tendencies that either productively maximize or detrimentally minimize the exercise of intelligence (see Figure I.1)

Furthermore, each of the "intelligence" stories presented in Chapters 3–8 is organized into three parts:

1. *The Story:* a brief account of relevant information about a particular dimension (i.e., physiological, social, emotional, constructive, reflective, dispositional) of the nature of human capacity for learning and achievement

Figure I.1   Six Dimensions of Intelligence

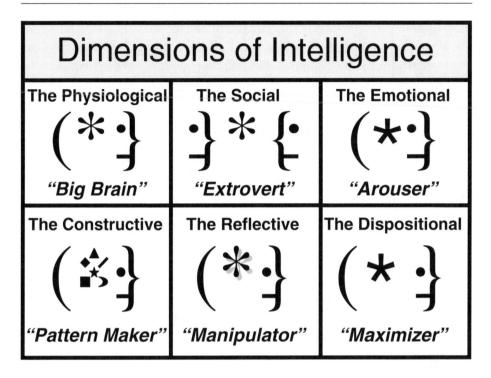

2. *The Meaning of the Story:* discernment of key aspects of human capacity that are particularly important to understand and attend to

3. *The Rest of the Story:* description of practical strategies and practices that nurture capacity in individuals and groups

In this fashion, the telling of the six stories reveals findings from an ongoing scientific journey of discovery—the exploration of the very headwaters of human capacity. Most important, given the performance focus of Part Two, each story concludes with descriptions of *mindful* (i.e., attentive) strategies and practices aligned to a specific dimension of intelligence. The practices presented at the end of Chapters 3–8 (i.e., 15–30 per chapter) are each organized and described by the following template:

The Practice: *What* the practice or activity is commonly called

The Place: *When* and *where* the practice might be applied

The Process: *How* the practice is conducted

The Payoff: *Why* the practice is of value to individual and group capacity

Each practice thus described is also coded by an assessment of its primary (black), secondary (gray), and associated (white) influence on the physiological (P), social (S), emotional (E), constructive (C), reflective (R), or dispositional (D) nature of intelligence capacity. For example, an assessment of a practice emphasizing reflection with secondary engagement of dispositional and social intelligence would be coded as follows:

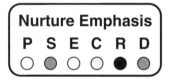

Part Three: Persistence

Part Three employs five scenarios to project an organizational culture that is intelligence informed and normed. It projects the perceptions and practices of a leader who is tightly connected to organizational purpose and the nature and nurture of human capacity. It also anticipates what might emerge when knowledge breakthroughs inform, leaders perform, and actions transform—that is, an intelligence-connected culture that maximizes organizational capacity for learning and achievement. Similar to reader reflections embedded throughout Part One and Part Two, this projection also encourages the reader to interpret content in the context of his or her personal leadership experience.

A Passionate Perspective

The ability to conceive an unlimited number of new combinations of ideas is the powerhouse of human intelligence and a key to our success as a species.

—Pinker (2002, p. 236)

This is a time in which leaders can and must lead with the brain in mind. The need for intelligence-informed leadership is great and, given recent scientific revelations, it is no longer excusable for leaders to either ignore or abuse the wealth of intelligence capacity that resides in any human system. Accordingly, four strong concerns about the status and requirements of twenty-first century leadership guide the contents of this book:

1.   Leadership must move on to a new paradigm. The advantages of intelligence-connected leadership have been unfolding for a long time through discriminating studies of successful individuals, organizations, and cultures (e.g., as referenced in Chapters 1–9). Old paradigms do die hard, but current breakthroughs in knowledge about human capacity nail the coffin lid on top-down leadership and other outmoded models and practices. Accordingly, leaders who remain unaware and uninformed about the nature and nurture of intelligence are as likely to create problems as they are to facilitate solutions and achievements.

2.   There are too many "lists" and "recipes" in the leadership literature and not enough "how to" directions for acting on credible research and theory. Practical example and experience is essential to the construction of any new knowledge, skill, or disposition. This is key to making a leap from informed perception to informed practice. Specifically, the leader who conceptually grasps new insights about the nature of intelligence might not, when left to his or her own means, figure out how to most effectively nurture it in either self or others. It is wise, then, to start leaders down that road through direct experience with practical, research-based practices that nurture learning and achievement.

3.   As Paul Simon advised, "there must be fifty ways to leave your lover." That is, the brain is capable of figuring out multiple approaches to resolving any challenge it faces. The 15 strategies and 100-plus practices presented in this book, then, are only examples to be considered by the force located above the eyes and between the ears. There is no conclusive list or recipe for influencing human achievement. Leaders must actively construct their leadership practice.

4.   Leadership is leadership is leadership and a brain is a brain is a brain. Leadership and intelligence are universal phenomena, and the interaction between the two is equally important in education, business, medicine, law, protective services, politics, government, sports, the military, and other human endeavors. There could hardly be a more appropriate environment for leading with the brain in mind than that of a school or classroom, but leaders in all fields have cause to be more tightly aligned to human capacity in thought and deed. They must, of course, examine such alignment in their particular contexts. It is also important, however, that leaders reach across professions to access a greater wealth of knowledge and experience—and greater perspective of universal best practices.

Part One

Perception

Leaders are well advised to be mindful of breakthroughs

in knowledge about the human brain and the intelligence it

enables. Emerging revelations about human capacity to learn

and achieve provide insight as to how one might best influence

the exercise of such capacity – both in self and others.

Accordingly, the wealth of information now emanating from

brain-intelligence research and theory is valuable to all who

are in a position to influence the life success of others.

1

The Connection

While the brain is but one organ among many in the human body, it is the source and the determiner of everything. Our understanding of the world changes in concert with the evolution of this delicate structure, which is unlike anything in the universe. Indeed, we understand the world the way we do at each of life's stages because of our brain. And yet, until lately, the brain jealously guarded its secrets. Only recently—with the development of powerful technologies—have we been successful in delving into the secrets of the Brain.

—Grubin (Restak, 2001, p. xvi)

The View From the Edge

The leadership connection to others has always traveled neural pathways because leadership is a phenomenon of the brain. At the edge of the twenty-first century, moreover, it is a connection that can and must be tightened. To involve your brain more directly regarding this point, reflect for a moment about whether the twenty-first century will: (1) become increasingly more challenging and complex, (2) expect and require more of human intelligence, and (3) place ever greater demands on leadership knowledge and skill.

Similar to completing a customs questionnaire when traveling abroad, your responses to the above projections were likely quick and consistent. It is fairly safe to assume that you anticipate a challenging future that will further raise the premium on the exercise of intelligence and leadership. This is not to suggest a pessimistic outlook, only what any informed adult living at this time in history might reasonably conclude—that the challenges that lie ahead will continually ask more of intelligence and leadership, rather than less.

Suffice it to say that early indicators suggest a bumpy ride. There is an ongoing threat of terrorism and war involving weapons of mass destruction. Scientific breakthroughs press issues of ethics and effects. The global economy suffers from political unrest, failed diplomacy, mismanagement, and greed. The environment continues to warm from abuses of production and consumption. Social and economic injustices strain political systems. Educational structures and programs are increasingly viewed as antiquated and inadequate. And, as if there was not enough on the agenda, our disposition to probe all facets of the universe continues to lure us into new explorations.

Is the future intimidating? Will humankind progress and prevail? At the edge of a future that only promises more complexity, is leadership as presently understood and practiced up to the task? It is with such questions in mind that a leader might pursue a tighter connection to the capacities that enable all human learning and achievement.

The Connection

> *More than anyone else, the boss creates the conditions that directly determine people's ability to work well.*
>
> —Goleman, Boyatzis,
> and McKee (2002, p. 18)

Leadership assumes a connection between leaders and others. It matters not who is the leader or what is the cause. One might look to the conquests of Alexander the Great or the humanitarian impact of Mother Teresa. Examples are as easily found in the everyday leadership of parents, teachers, coaches, clerics, politicians, and corporate officers. In every case, leadership is defined by a connection with others that produces results.

At its core, moreover, the leadership connection to others is a matter of influence and context—and the present context is providing extraordinary insight into the neural nature of the influence. This is the heart of the matter, the point that must not be lost if a deeper understanding of leadership is to be realized. *The brain has everything to do with who we are and what we do, and leadership is all about influencing who we are and what we do.* Thus, the leadership connection to others necessarily travels neural pathways.

A Matter of Influence

Leadership is a process of influencing others toward the achievement of a goal (Dickmann & Stanford-Blair, 2002). Numerous attempts to interpret

Figure 1.1 Elements of Leadership: A Process of Influencing Others Toward the Achievement of a Goal.

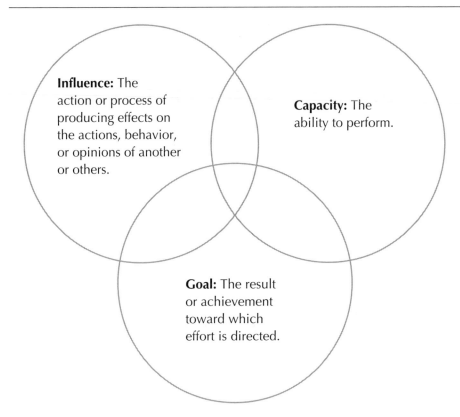

Influence: The action or process of producing effects on the actions, behavior, or opinions of another or others.

Capacity: The ability to perform.

Goal: The result or achievement toward which effort is directed.

the nature of the phenomenon have produced many versions of this basic understanding. Most, nevertheless, acknowledge a fundamental process of influence occurring between two or more individuals toward the achievement of a goal (e.g., Burns, 1978; Rost, 1991; Northouse, 1997). Furthermore, while goals range and change, the basic elements of the process remain the same. Leadership—whether exercised by presidents or parents, individuals or groups—is always about developing, encouraging, facilitating, or otherwise influencing the capacity of others toward the achievement of a goal (see Figure 1.1).

This definitional matter is important to the content that follows for three reasons. First, it values clarity about goals. Second, it prompts leaders to pursue productive relationships with others (i.e., acknowledging that the leader cannot go it alone). Third, it implies that a leader should know a thing or two about the nature (i.e., the capacity) of the other(s) they aspire to influence. Indeed, it is this third point that encourages twenty-first-century leaders to access emerging knowledge about the nature of intelligence.

A Matter of Context

The leadership process stays the same while the goals range and change, but context directs the game. Change is a constant in nature and human systems. Abruptly or methodically, contexts inevitably shift, and so does leadership in response. Leaders adapt *how* they influence others to the context in which their influence is attempted. Accordingly, brute strength worked to influence others in the historical context of the cave. Similarly, the rule of the enlightened few over the ignorant masses fit the context of medieval times. There is little tolerance and even less rationale, however, for brutes and monarchs in modern history. Educated populations and sophisticated technologies create a context that favors brain over brawn and democracy over dictatorship. It is a context in which leaders influence others by communicating the merits of an idea or action—often employing sophisticated technologies in doing so. The phenomenon of leadership, then, is always a process of influencing others to achieve a goal, but the exercise of such influence must adapt to the context in which it is being exercised.

Case in point, emerging knowledge about the nature of intelligence holds promise for new understanding about how leaders might more effectively influence others toward goal achievement. It is a contextual opportunity born of scientific breakthroughs that are revealing the secrets of the brain and, thereby, opening the heretofore "black box" of intelligence. It is an extraordinary opportunity to know how the brain enables the capacities that leaders aspire to employ and influence—to understand the intelligence base that underlies all human ability to perform and achieve (see Figure 1.2.).

The importance of this context-enabled opportunity for a better understanding of the leadership connection to the brain might be all too obvious to some. It might also be a relationship, however, that is less understood and appreciated by most. After all, leaders might effectively influence others with only an intuitive sense of how their behavior is being processed through the brains of the group. Furthermore, meaningful scientific revelations about the nature of the brain and its intelligence qualities are of relatively recent vintage. Accordingly, a leader might be forgiven for not being steeped in knowledge about the nature and importance of the leadership-brain connection.

Tolerance of such ignorance, nonetheless, is inevitably limited by the leadership demands of the twenty-first century context—a context that calls for more effective alignment of leadership influence to the nature of human capacity for achieving compelling goals.

The brain is the immediate force behind who we are and what we do, and leadership is about influencing who we are and what we do. Accordingly, leaders necessarily influence others through neural pathways because the

Figure 1.2 Perception of Intelligence as the Foundation of Capacity in the Leadership Process.

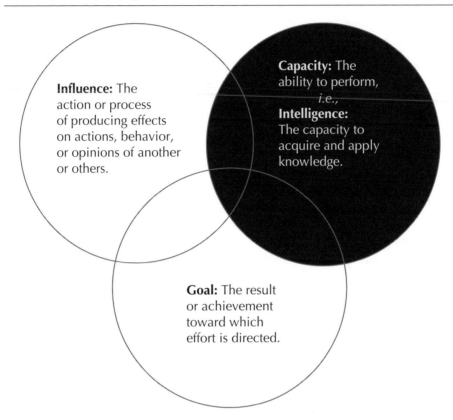

Influence: The action or process of producing effects on actions, behavior, or opinions of another or others.

Capacity: The ability to perform, *i.e.,*
Intelligence: The capacity to acquire and apply knowledge.

Goal: The result or achievement toward which effort is directed.

brain enables the multidimensional capacities that leaders connect to in self and others. There is no choice in this matter. Such connection inevitably occurs, whether intuitively or consciously, because qualities of intelligence are the means by which the brain creates mind and connects to other brains.

In summary, leadership influence on human capacity has historically relied on intuition and insight gained from trial and error. Breakthroughs in knowledge about the nature of human intelligence present an opportunity to alter that circumstance. More mindful (i.e., attentive) alignment of the leadership process that marshals human resources toward the achievement of desired results is now possible. The knowledge of the twenty-first century enables a tightening of the leadership connection to the intelligence capacity that underlies all human achievement. It is a breakthrough opportunity that projects capacity-connected leaders—leaders who are more aligned in perception and practice to how individuals and groups best learn and achieve goals (see Figure 1.3).

Figure 1.3   Mindful Alignment of Leadership Influence to Capacity and Purpose

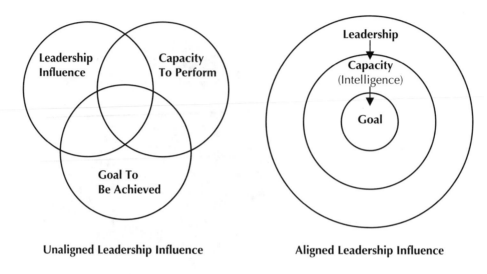

Unaligned Leadership Influence   Aligned Leadership Influence

Reader Reflection

1. What is leadership?

2. What is intelligence?

3. What is the relationship between leadership and intelligence?

2

The Connected Leader

Clearly, these are exciting times—there is a lot going on. Not the least of these developments is the new realization that leadership is the key to large-scale improvement yet must be radically different than it ever has been before. Further, effective leadership is in very short supply. We can therefore expect to see leadership initiatives dominating the scene over the next decade.

—Fullan (2001, p. xii)

The Tighter Connection

Leaders are disposed to cross the frontiers that they encounter in life. They venture beyond awareness to construct new realities. They bridge knowledge to action. What might leaders know and do, then, if they sought and found how to be more tightly connected to human capacity in perception and practice? The following sections preview such connections in anticipation of the stories and examples described in Chapters 3–8.

Connected in Perception

Everyone has a theory of human nature. Everyone has to anticipate the behaviors of others, and that means we all need theories about what makes people tick.

—Pinker (2002, p. 1)

With reference to a convergence of scientific knowledge, a leader can now realize a more informed perception of human nature. Aware of the fundamental qualities of intelligence that underlie the ability to learn and perform, a leader's influence on others is positioned to be more foundational, comprehensive, and effective. To that end, a capacity-connected leader (who we will refer to here as Alexis to put flesh on the concept) will cultivate essential perceptions about what empowers all human learning and achievement. She will understand that intelligence—the capacity to acquire and apply knowledge—operates in multiple dimensions in the brain. For example, as an intelligence-informed leader, Alexis will know that

1. **Intelligence is a physiological process:** The capacity to learn and achieve operates on a biological platform of cells, circuits, and chemicals in the brain. It is a platform that is *big, mind-body connected, high maintenance, and malleable*. Virtually unlimited in its capacity for processing information, the brain is the body and the body is the brain. What affects one affects the other. To do its work well, then, the brain demands both quantity and quality in nutritional care and environmental experience. Most important, the brain's neural networks are modified by experience. Neural plasticity in learning continues throughout the lifespan. Thus, the nature of brain capacity for acquiring and applying knowledge (i.e., intelligence) is not fixed but malleable by environmental nurture.

2. **Intelligence is a social process:** Born of rich social experience over millions of years, the human brain is endowed with *hyper-social instincts*—natural and powerful abilities for memory, language, empathy, sympathy, collaboration, and reasoning. Indeed, the brain's social bias is such that it is socially *expectant, dependent, extended, and oriented to virtue*. The unfolding of brain capacity for learning and achievement is expectant of the same social experience that constructed it. Social experience, moreover, is the great provocateur of the quality of thinking and learning that the brain depends on to realize its potential. To satisfy this overarching need and disposition for interaction in a society of mind, the brain has invented a variety of media that extend social interaction beyond face-to-face encounters (e.g., art, writing, print, telephone, radio, film, television, and the Internet). The brain also has an instinctive social sense of virtue as demonstrated by its moral orientation to pro-social behavior.

3. ***Intelligence is an emotional process:*** Emotion moves the brain to *attention, judgment, motivation,* and reasoned *management* of mind-body states. It involves neural and glandular systems that trigger changes in mind and body in response to evaluations of external and internal information—reflexive changes that arouse brain attention to what is important. Classic examples of emotion-triggered mind-body states are fear, anger, joy, sorrow, surprise, and disgust. The reflexive arousal systems associated with emotion initiate immediate and automatic responses to environmental stimulation (i.e., fight or flight). Subsequently, emotional centers interact with rational reasoning systems in the brain to judge the merits of events and available options. Emotion also plays a role in motivation by arousing and sustaining passion about things that matter. Furthermore, emotion represents a brain-body function that is manageable, but only after the fact. The brain is able to recognize and mediate emotional responses after they occur—a capacity referred to as emotional intelligence.

4. ***Intelligence is a constructive process:*** The fundamental genius of the human brain is its capacity for constructing useful information patterns. It is an ability that is *sensory, social, emotional, and reflective*—but also susceptible to *a double bind.* The brain is a "lean, mean, pattern-making machine," a biological platform of extraordinary capacity for constructing meaning and memory from divers information sources. It constructs knowledge of the world from sensory input stimulated by environmental experience—and direct, rich experience influences the quality of such construction. Social interaction is a primary source for rich environmental experiences, but emotion also plays an important role in the construction of what the brain understands and remembers. The brain is aroused and sustained in its attention to knowledge constructions that are emotionally judged to be worthy of the time and effort. The construction of meaning and memory is further facilitated by rich emotional contexts that reference the organization of important information patterns. What is constructed and remembered, moreover, is continually refined and reconstructed by the brain through ongoing examination of relationships to new information. The brain has to be wary of a double bind, nevertheless, as comfort with existing information patterns can engender disregard for the value of new information.

5. ***Intelligence is a reflective process:*** The crowning glory of the human brain is exhibited in its reflective capacity. It is a capacity that

is *manipulative, executive, governing, unifying, and promising* in nature. Reflection is the distinguishing brain capacity for consciously manipulating information and rehearsing options prior to action— to move beyond the construction of what is to reconstructions of what has been and projections of what might be. To do this, the reflective process incorporates an executive function that purposefully accesses, coordinates, and directs the vast resources of the brain in the exercise of complex reasoning. Reflection also performs a governing role as it constrains, redirects, or otherwise remedies actions initiated in other brain areas—particularly actions initiated in the emotional centers of the brain. Furthermore, reflective attention to a meaningful problem or decision has a unifying effect on other dimensions of intelligence. For example, problem solving and decision making require physiological support, social interaction, emotional tension, knowledge construction, and productive dispositions. Ultimately, reflection is the most promising of human capacities as expressed in scientific inquiry, philosophy, and art. It is the capacity that empowers human versatility and, thereby, all future prospects.

6. **Intelligence is a dispositional process:** The brain is disposed to exercise its intelligence capacities in a manner that is *macro, mandatory, malleable,* and either *maximizing or minimizing.* The brain adopts macro patterns of thinking called dispositions (i.e., mental tendencies or inclinations) that are habitually applied on a broad scale as the brain goes about its business. For purposes of efficiency and effectiveness in the allocation of its considerable resources, the brain has no option other than to develop and exercise habits of thinking. There are quality options for the brain to consider, however, as habits of mind are malleable. That is, thinking dispositions are genetically introduced and environmentally influenced. The conscious cultivation of good thinking habits is critical, therefore, because such dispositions are determining factors in how far and well one travels the neural byways of the brain. Human capacity to think, learn, and achieve is realized to the degree to which there is a productive disposition driving it.

7. **Intelligence is an integrated process:** It is helpful to break down the intelligence capacity of the brain into digestible pieces, but the brain exercises its multidimensional capacity for acquiring and applying knowledge in a highly integrated manner. The various

dimensions of intelligence have evolved together, are dependent on one another, and are designed to work in concert. Accordingly, if one dimension of intelligence is restricted or incapacitated in some manner, all other dimensions suffer markedly in efficiency and effect.

Is it important for Alexis to be thus informed about the nature of human capacity? The answer to that question is of consequence to the leadership that will evolve in the twenty-first century. It is an answer, moreover, to be constructed in the brains of individual leaders.

In reflecting about this matter, you will advisedly reject the idea that ignorance is bliss. It is more certain that knowledge is power and that what you don't know might hurt you or others. Is it important for a leader to be informed about the multidimensional nature of intelligence? Consider Alexis's prospects if she is uninformed about how the brain works. Unaware of the nature of brain-enabled intelligence, her attempts to influence others toward the achievement of a goal might be visualized as shooting in the dark and at great risk of being misdirected or repelled. That is not to say that as an intuitive leader Alexis would not often do the right thing and adequately connect with others to get the job done. Rather, the issue is how as an intelligence-informed leader she might realize some advantage in influencing human capacity toward the achievement of goals. From that view, being connected in perception to the nature of capacity is a prerequisite to more effectively connecting to that capacity in practice (see Figure 2.1).

Connected in Practice

Look at the world around you. It may seem like an immovable, implacable place. It is not. With the slightest push—in just the right place—it can be tipped.

—Gladwell (2000, p. 259)

The cultivation of informed perception is one part of leading with the brain in mind. It involves building a foundation of credible knowledge about how the brain performs its work. The next important step for Alexis is translating what she knows about capacity into what she does about capacity. That is, she must align strategies and practices to informed perceptions if she

Figure 2.1   The Advantage of Capacity-Connected Leadership

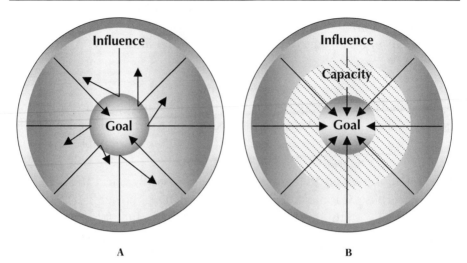

A. Uninformed about the nature of intelligence capacity, leadership behavior employs intuitive trial and error influence on others to achieve a goal.

B. Informed about the nature of intelligence capacity, leadership behavior is more effectively connected to that capacity in influencing others toward the achievement of a goal.

is to realize any advantage in her influence on others. For example, seeking to organize such alignment Alexis might reflect that

- Given my *perception* that intelligence operates on a biological platform of cells, circuits, and chemicals, my *strategy* is to nurture brain fitness through *practices* that promote movement, nutrition, humor, and novelty.
- Given my *perception* that social experience is the great provocateur of thinking and learning, my *strategy* is to facilitate social interaction through *practices* that promote thinking in waves, pairs, triads, progressions, and alliances.
- Given my *perception* that emotion is the means by which the brain attends, judges, and is motivated, my *strategy* is to harness the power of emotion through *practices* that promote norms, affirmation, mission, and conflict resolution.
- Given my *perception* that the brain is a lean, mean pattern-making machine, my *strategy* is to facilitate the construction of meaning through *practices* that promote assessment and review, sensory engagement, questioning, and coaching.

Figure 2.2   A Framework for Connecting Leadership to the Brain

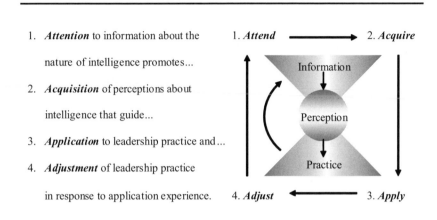

1. *Attention* to information about the nature of intelligence promotes...

2. *Acquisition* of perceptions about intelligence that guide...

3. *Application* to leadership practice and...

4. *Adjustment* of leadership practice in response to application experience.

- Given my *perception* that the brain reflectively manipulates information and options prior to action, my *strategy* is to structure thinking through *practices* that promote storming, norming, debating, analyzing, projecting, solving, and creating.
- Given my *perception* that thinking dispositions maximize the exercise of intelligence, my *strategy* is to target productive habits of mind through *practices* that promote listening, open mindedness, clarity, persistence, and collaboration.

Herein lies the challenge and task at hand—to bridge informed leadership perception (i.e., understanding) of human capacity to compatible leadership practice (i.e., habitual performance). Such bridging, moreover, assumes some structured effort.

A prior work, *Connecting Leadership to the Brain* (Dickmann & Stanford-Blair, 2002), proposed a framework for organizing and applying breakthrough information about human intelligence. A portion of that triune structure is useful to the bridgework that lies ahead in Chapters 3–8 (see Figure 2.2). It is a framework by which a leader can connect knowledge to action. Given the attention to capacity-connected leadership in these first two chapters, that framework will now be employed within the format of short stories about specific dimensions of intelligence across the next six chapters.

Each story will directly connect perceptions of the nature of capacity to practical practices that nurture it in individuals and groups. To that end, each chapter will feature strategies and practices that model *leading with the brain in mind*. The six stories will also associate human characters (e.g., Alexis) with conceptual content to foster reality connections to leadership contexts (e.g., to the people you work with). Indeed, the intent of this format is to help leaders better understand and appreciate what makes people tick—and what they might do to synchronize their influence to the powerful nature of that neural ticking.

Reader Reflection

1. What is the advantage of "capacity-connected" leadership?

2. Why is it important to align intelligence-informed leadership perception to intelligence-informed leadership practice?

Part Two

Performance

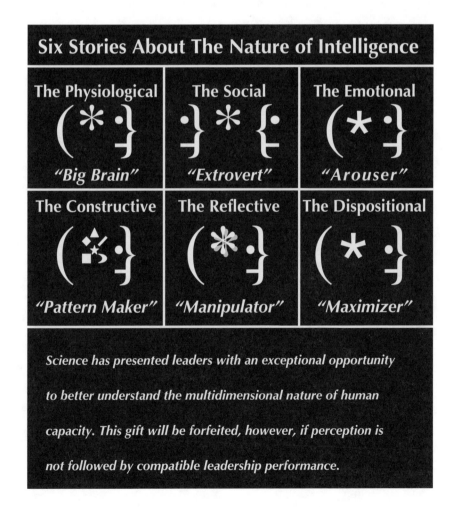

Six Stories About The Nature of Intelligence

The Physiological	The Social	The Emotional
(*•}	•}*{•	(*•}
"Big Brain"	*"Extrovert"*	*"Arouser"*
The Constructive	The Reflective	The Dispositional
(•}	(*•}	(*•}
"Pattern Maker"	*"Manipulator"*	*"Maximizer"*

Science has presented leaders with an exceptional opportunity to better understand the multidimensional nature of human capacity. This gift will be forfeited, however, if perception is not followed by compatible leadership performance.

3

Physiological Nature and Nurture

The Story of Physiological Capacity

Brian has a big brain. As a normal, healthy human being, he is endowed with an exceptionally large, complex, and capable brain. This is the story of Brian's big brain—a story about a big break, a big platform, a big connection, and a big advantage. It is an account, moreover, that provides background for the stories that follow in Chapters 4–8.

The Big Break

Approximately 2.5 million years ago, one of the already more advanced brains on Earth moved far ahead of other such brains. It advanced in such dramatic fashion that it reshaped the head that housed it. It not only moved ahead, it changed a head. The brain making that break to a larger size was that of Brian's early ancestors living on the savannahs of Africa. It was the evolutionary advent of the big brain that today truly differentiates Brian from other life on the planet.

What precipitated a dramatic advancement in human brain size? Some point to the development of a bipedal posture that facilitated the use of primitive tools and the scavenging of a high protein meat diet (Mithen, 1996). Others reference the challenges associated with sudden climate changes (Calvin, 2002). Many credit prolonged social experience for expanding a neural capacity for processing socially referenced information (Calvin, 1996; Gazzaniga, 1998; Pinker, 1997). Whatever the combination of causes, the brain that evolved was big in a way that counted. It was unmatched in capacity for doing the survival work that all brains do. It progressed far beyond the basic regulation of body systems and processing of environmental information. It was a brain equipped with the physiological capacity necessary for consciousness, language, and reflective reasoning.

The Big Platform

All brains are in the business of processing information to gain a survival advantage. They perform this function on biological platforms composed of cells, circuits, and chemicals. Brian's brain packs a big platform in a three-and-a-half-pound collection of physiological structures that regulate and operate all of his behavior.

Brian's brain is the major component of the central nervous system. It is a highly integrated system of structures commonly described as regions, hemispheres, lobes, areas, cells, and circuits. The *cerebrum* is the forebrain region that represents over 70% of Brian's brain (see Figure 3.1). This is the brain structure that makes his brain much bigger than that of other primates. It envelops most other brain structures and is divided into two hemispheres that collectively enable qualities of movement, comprehension, emotion, communication, logic, and creativity. The outer portion of the cerebrum is called the *cerebral cortex* (from Latin for *bark* or *rind*), a dense, deeply folded integration of neural brain cells less than a quarter of an inch in thickness. Each cortex hemisphere is organized into lobes, strips, and areas associated with particular brain functions.

Figure 3.1   Lateral and Top View of the Human Brain

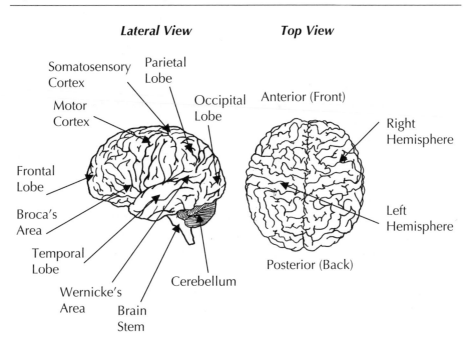

At the fore of each hemisphere is the *frontal lobe* associated with critical thinking, problem solving, creativity, and planning—the complex reasoning processes that most distinguish Brian's mental abilities. The reflective mediation of emotional responses is attributed to an interior region of this same area. *Broca's area* in the lower rear portion of the left frontal lobe (reversed to the right hemisphere in 5% of the population) is associated with the production of language—another distinguishing feature of Brian's mental capacity. Immediately behind the frontal lobe in each hemisphere is a strip called the *motor cortex*, which controls voluntary movement in the opposite side of the body. At the back of each hemisphere is the *occipital lobe*. This area has primary responsibility for processing visual information. The area of the brain above the occipital lobe is called the *parietal lobe*, which is involved in processing sensory information from the opposite side of the body.

A strip at the front of the parietal lobe and adjacent to the motor cortex is the *somatosensory cortex*, which receives feedback about pain, pressure, temperature, and touch. The *temporal lobe* above and around the ear area in each hemisphere assumes a primary responsibility for hearing as well as a role in memory and learning. *Wernicke's area* at the junction of the left temporal, occipital, and parietal lobes (again reversed to the right hemisphere in 5% of the population) is associated with speech comprehension and the organization of words in speaking, reading, and writing.

A medial view of Brian's brain reveals structures hidden beneath the mantel of the cerebral cortex (see Figure 3.2). The *hindbrain* emerges from the *spinal cord* (the other component of the central nervous system) and is composed of the medulla and pons—commonly referred to as the brain stem—and the cerebellum. The brain stem is a communication corridor for information exchanges between brain and body. A network of brain cells in this stem section form the *reticular formation* that regulates involuntary body motor activity such as heart rate, respiration, blood pressure, and gastrointestinal function. This formation is also involved in the regulation of brain arousal and consciousness in relation to changing environmental conditions. Such regulation operates subconsciously in the brain stem, thus relieving Brian's conscious brain from constant attention to basic life-support system management.

The *cerebellum* (Latin for *little brain*) is attached to the brain stem below the occipital lobes of the cerebral cortex. It is associated with movement, balance, and memory of "how to" procedures that become automatic, such as bike riding or multiplication tables. The cerebellum also interacts with the frontal cortex when movement facilitates thinking and learning—as when Brian moves to write, draw, act out, or verbally express what is in his head. The small *midbrain* area at the top of the brain stem mediates visual reflexes and coordinated head and eye movements important to processing visual information.

The medial perspective of Brian's dominating *forebrain* also reveals the communication arch of hundreds of millions of neural fibers in the *corpus callosum*, which bridges the two cerebral hemispheres. Other significant forebrain structures include

- The walnut size *thalamus* (from Greek for *chamber* or *inner room*) centered above the brain stem, which relays sensory and motor information to other areas of the brain for processing of what is happening outside Brian's body and what his body is doing. The *olfactory bulb* also relays sensory information to the brain.
- The thumbnail size *hypothalamus* located below the thalamus, which relays information about what is happening within Brian's body to other areas of the brain. It regulates basic drives and states such as temperature, sexual activity, and appetite. It also interacts with the pituitary gland to regulate body states and the medulla to regulate internal organs like the heart, lungs, and bladder.

Figure 3.2   Medial View of the Brain

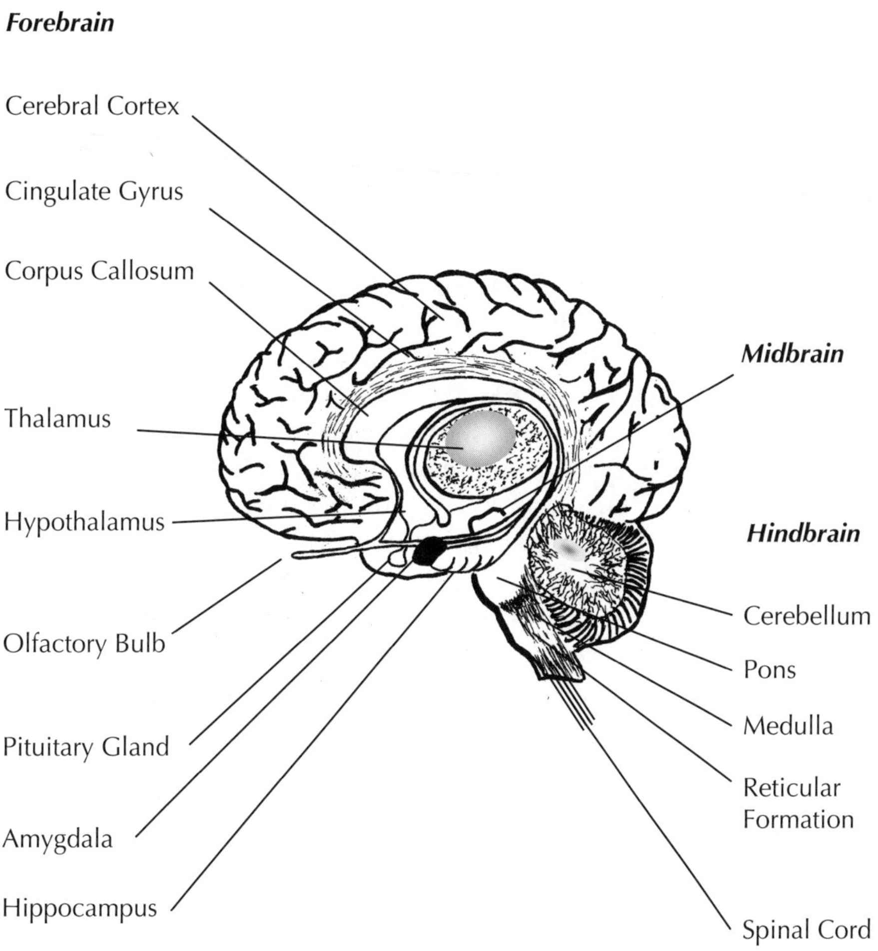

Forebrain

Cerebral Cortex

Cingulate Gyrus

Corpus Callosum

Midbrain

Thalamus

Hindbrain

Hypothalamus

Cerebellum

Olfactory Bulb

Pons

Medulla

Pituitary Gland

Reticular
Formation

Amygdala

Hippocampus

Spinal Cord

- The *pituitary gland* beneath the hypothalamus, which is regulated by hypothalamic neurons to release pituitary hormones into the bloodstream that in turn prompt the endocrine system to release other hormones that adjust body chemistry.
- The *hippocampus,* shaped like an upside down seahorse, which helps index information throughout Brian's brain, thereby enabling learning and memory formation.
- The almond size *amygdala* at the tip of the hippocampus, which processes sensory information in a way that integrates emotion with memory. It is one of a number of emotional centers in Brian's brain that triggers reflexive responses. It also arouses reflective reasoning to the management of emotional responses.

Knowing about Brian's basic brain structures and functions provides a big picture of a big platform for acquiring and applying information. The inside story about that platform, however, is one of communication at the cellular level—the exchanges of electrochemically coded information between billions of neurons that direct all behavior.

The *neuron* is the principal cellular unit in Brian's brain. The main components of a neural cell are the *cell body*, an output fiber called the *axon*, and multiple input fibers called *dendrites* (see Figure 3.3). Neural communication in Brian's brain occurs through networks of *synapse* exchange sites between the dendrite and axon fibers emanating from neurons. It is at these sites that electric impulses from cell bodies cause axons to release *neurotransmitters* (chemicals) to the dendrite receptor sites of other neurons.

Simply stated, neurons are the communication agents in Brian's brain. Those agents "talk" to each other through exchanges of electrochemically coded information. You can visualize the process by looking at your right hand and arm. The palm of your hand represents the body cell of a neuron. Your fingers and thumb represent the dendrite extensions. When the dendrites receive a chemically coded message from a synapse interaction with another neuron (wiggle your fingers), that code generates the firing of an electrical impulse from ion exchanges in the cell body (arch the palm of your hand). That impulse is then conducted by the axon as an *action potential* to its terminal ports (follow the movement of the impulse from the palm of your hand to the tip of your elbow) where it causes the release of select chemicals into a synapse between the axon terminal and a dendrite of another neuron (wiggle the fingers of your left hand next to your right elbow). Thus the conversation continues from neuron to neuron in Brian's brain.

While the above process may be simply visualized, it is much more difficult to comprehend in its full complexity and capacity. Brian's brain houses a communication community of an estimated 100 billion neurons concentrated in layers and columns in the cerebral cortex and nuclei clusters in other brain structures (areas so richly composed of dark neural cells that they present the appearance of "gray matter"). The work of neural cells is supported by an estimated one trillion *glial* (from Greek for "glue") cells that provide organization, nutrition, and maintenance services for neurons in Brian's brain. It is glial cells that form insulating *myelin* sheaths (the "white matter" of the brain) around the axons of neurons to enhance the efficiency of communication between neurons throughout Brian's brain. Thus supported, neurons utilize nerve fibers and hormone transmissions in the blood stream to communicate with the entire body system.

Figure 3.3   Components and Communications of Neural Cells

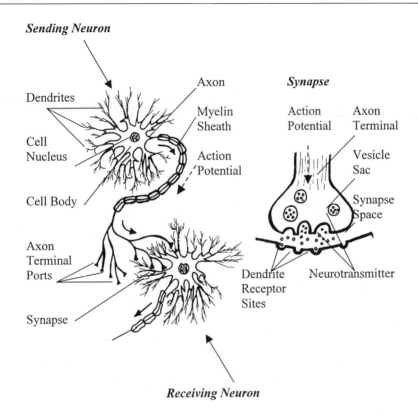

Sending Neuron

Dendrites

Cell
Nucleus

Cell Body

Axon
Terminal
Ports

Synapse

Axon

Myelin
Sheath

Action
Potential

Synapse

Action   Axon
Potential   Terminal

Vesicle
Sac

Synapse
Space

Dendrite   Neurotransmitter
Receptor
Sites

Receiving Neuron

Consider further that tens of thousands of neurons can fit on the head of a pin and that a single neuron may utilize hundreds of dendritic branches to simultaneously communicate with tens of thousands of other neurons (picture a conference call with as many people), each of which is linked to a like number of other neurons within a collective network that approximates a quadrillion (a million billion) neural connections. This multitude of connections employs a vast array of neurotransmitters that do the actual communication footwork (e.g., *epinephrine* and *norepinephrine* direct stress responses and arousal of alertness, *dopamine* communicates body movement and positive moods or pleasure, *serotonin* regulates mood and sleep, *acetylcholine* modulates muscular movement and memory formation, and *endorphins* are associated with pain reduction and feelings of pleasure and euphoria). The action also takes place at a fast pace in Brian's brain with action impulses traveling down axons at estimated speeds of 200 miles per hour—which is virtually instantaneous, given the distance covered. When you put it all together, it's an extraordinary neural platform for processing information and learning.

The Big Connection

The big platform is connected to the body in a big way. That is, Brian's brain and body are one integrated system. His brain is his body and his body is his brain, because what happens to one affects the other. For example, if Brian's brain is engaged in reflection about a worrisome problem, the digestive processes in his stomach and the respiratory activity in his lungs will become aware of and adjust to that mental activity (e.g., a queasy stomach and shallow breathing). If Brian's stomach is upset from the intake of too much pizza or his lungs are stressed from a long run, his brain will be aware of such circumstance and initiate action accordingly (e.g., take an antacid or seek to rest).

The integration of mind and body is particularly important to how Brian learns. That is, intelligence is not the product of the brain alone. As Hannaford (1995) has observed, the body's senses provide the information from which the brain forms its understanding of the world. Physical movement, moreover, activates neural wiring throughout the body, making the entire body system the instrument of learning. For this reason, there is a natural kinesthetic quality to Brian's neural processing of information.

It is quite obvious that Brian's brain has a reciprocal arrangement with his body. It is a physiological system within a physiological system. The brain is responsible for the welfare of the body and is in turn dependent on the body for its welfare. This mind-body relationship is evident in the maintenance requirements of Brian's brain.

Brian's brain consumes approximately 20% of his body energy in operating and maintaining its neural networks. This is a high demand from a biological system representing 2% of body weight. Such energy in the form of oxygen, glucose, protein, and trace elements arrives in the blood richly supplied by the carotid artery.

As to important sources of nutrition for Brian's brain needs, a mother's traditional advice remains sound: lean meats, fish (salmon and tuna are highly recommended), eggs, dairy products (e.g., yogurt), nuts, whole grains, and fresh fruits (particularly citrus fruits and bananas) and vegetables (leafy greens, beans, and carrots in particular). Hydration is another important nutrition concern because the composition of the brain is approximately 78% water. Water is also integral to the digestive and respiratory processes that provide oxygen and other energy sources to his brain.

Accordingly, Brian's brain requires regular hydration from the consumption of water (about eight glasses a day).

The physiological maintenance of Brian's brain further benefits from blood oxygenation through exercise, regular exposure to light (preferably natural), fresh air, and rest. His brain also needs relief from the extended presence of demanding neurotransmitters in its myriad synapses. The excessive involvement of chemical agents such as epinephrine, norepinephrine, and seratonin can cause undue wear and tear on the brain—or simply gum up the works. Thus, it is important for Brian to regularly exercise, follow a good diet, smile, laugh, rest, and otherwise affect positive chemical states of mind (Gage, 2003). To that same end, he must avoid abusive consumption of substances (e.g., sugar, fats, cigarettes, alcohol) that impair the finely structured physical operations of his brain.

The Big Advantage

Each human brain, absent significant developmental miscues or physical trauma, is a powerful physiological platform for information processing. It is a brain, moreover, that is shaped by experience. That is, Brian's neural networks evolve throughout his lifespan. His intelligence capacity is not fixed but malleable by the quality and quantity of environmental experience he encounters. Indeed, a defining characteristic of his brain is the expanse of neural circuitry that is undedicated and environmentally responsive. Concentrated in the cerebral "gray matter" of the brain, such networks respond to novel situations and continually accommodate new understanding.

This is a critical point to appreciate about Brian's brain. The neural development initiated in the womb will continue until his death. His young brain engaged in the generation and restructuring of neural networks that were timely to early developmental events in his life, such as mastery of visual and auditory acuity, bipedal mobility, language, and abstract thinking. The principle behind such neural growth was and is that networks that are stimulated and productive are networks that are promoted and supported. A neuron will commit to associations with other neurons if there is genetic direction or environmental stimulation to do so. Thus, modification of neural networking is *always* occurring in Brian's brain, both prior to and following the development of his mature adult brain at about age 16. It involves bifurcation (branching) of dendrites and myelination of axons extending from the neurons that originated in the womb. This growth of "bushy" dendrites and myelinated axons physically refines the gray and white matter in Brian's brain. The really good news is that this trait of neural modifiability, often called *plasticity*, is lifelong. In effect, Brian's brain is never complete.

Studies conducted by Greenough and Black (1992) and others have firmly established the positive effect of environmental enrichment on dendrite branching, synapse formation, and axon myelination in animals of all ages. Investigations of the effects of aging on the mental acuity of human subjects by Schaie and Willis (1986) and Snowden (2001) are representative studies that draw the same conclusion: Capacity to develop and reconfigure neural networks throughout the life span is strongly correlated to the richness of environmental experience. Factors that enrich Brian's neural plasticity include level of education, physical activity, participation in professional and cultural activities, perception of accomplishment, and association with smart people.

It's a pretty good deal. Brian is given a genetic endowment of more neurons than he needs plus the capacity to continually refine what he is given. The physiological base of his intelligence is factory installed but remains perpetually under construction.

The Meaning of the Story

The bottom line about Brian's big brain is what it enables. A qualified computer analogy is useful to this point—qualified by the fact that no computer (at this point in time) is biological in nature or anywhere near as complex and capable as Brian's brain. Given that caveat, you are undoubtedly aware of the advantage of a computer platform that accommodates rapid processing and storage of large amounts of information. Such capacity underlies all subsequent computer functions and services. You may purchase and attempt to employ any number of additional features—all the bells and whistles—but if the information capacity is not there, things either will work poorly or not at all. The physiology of Brian's brain, then, can be thought of as the platform of enormous capacity that enables and operates all other dimensions of intelligence. It is much more profound than that, however, in that the size and capacity that support the social, emotional, constructive, reflective, and dispositional dimensions of intelligence are themselves a product and a beneficiary of those same capacities. The exercise of that which physiological capacity enables in turn nurtures greater physiological capacity.

One might necessarily conclude that nature has composed the most complex and productive creation in the universe within Brian's head. Moreover, if not maintained and operated as nature intends, that creation will neither support nor realize its potential.

What, then, is the meaning of Brian's story? Dare a leader dismiss the physical underpinnings of human intelligence? And if not, what is most important to know about the physiological brain? The answer to those questions must ultimately be constructed in the leader's brain. To facilitate the construction of such perspective, nevertheless, several statements about the essential nature of physiological capacity follow—summary perceptions of a brain that is big, mind-body connected, high maintenance, and malleable.

Big

Human intelligence is physiologically enabled—it operates on a biological platform of cells, circuits, and chemicals that is virtually unlimited in its capacity for processing information. The physical capacity of Brian's brain for productively acquiring and applying knowledge exceeds what most people, including Brian, might normally appreciate. The danger is not that Brian's brain will be required to process and organize more than it can handle, but rather that it will be underutilized.

Mind-Body Connected

The brain is the body and the body is the brain, and what affects one affects the other. Brian's body is a highly integrated extension of his brain. The entire physiology—hands, heart, stomach, and everything else—is intimately engaged in the work of the brain. Information processing is not limited to the body region between the ears and behind the eyes. The brain is in an information-processing partnership with the body.

High Maintenance

To do its work well, the brain demands both quantity and quality in nutritional care and environmental experience. The advantages of the most complex brain on the planet come at a price. Brian's neural business requires maintenance and stimulation.

Malleable

Neural networks in the brain are modified by experience, and plasticity in learning continues throughout the lifespan—intelligence capacity is not fixed, but malleable by the quality and quantity of environmental experience encountered. Brian's brain is a work in progress. Dendrites will branch and axons will strengthen by virtue of experience.

The Rest of the Story

Describing a physically big, connected, demanding, and malleable brain sets the stage for the rest of the story: an account of what might be done to nurture what nature provides. Such reflection might first acknowledge that one usually attends to possessions of value. Brian's car, for example, has the capacity to transport him in comfort and safety to distant places over many years and thousands of miles. Not much of what his car is designed to do is going to happen, however, unless the oil is changed, the tank filled, the tires rotated, and the battery recharged or replaced—not to mention interior and exterior cleaning for reasons of emotional ambiance. Similarly, Brian's computer can connect him to a world of information, but that will not as likely happen either unless he is attentive to power sources, software updates, server links, and virus protections.

Given such care and attention to valued technologies, it would seem reasonable that one might attend to the organ that underlies every quality of what it means to be human—our big brain. To that end, one must organize aligned strategies and practices.

Mindful Strategy

With reference to the physiological nature of the brain in Brian's head, what might a leader do to nurture such capacity in self and others? Two strategies follow.

Strategy: Attend to Brain Fitness

The information-processing capacity of the brain is enabled by a biological platform of cells, circuits, and chemicals that is dependant on care from its host body. Accordingly, a leader will attend to brain fitness through exercise, nutrition, and fun.

Strategy: Stimulate Neural Networks

Neural networks continue to develop throughout the lifespan according to quality and quantity of environmental experience. Accordingly, a leader will engineer social interaction, meaningful challenge, novelty, and rich sensory stimulation.

Mindful Practice

Describing the physical nature of Brian's brain opens the story. Consideration of strategies that are mindful of such capacity moves the story to the edge of action. A good story, however, requires a strong ending. Thus, this story concludes with practices one might employ to nurture physiological capacity for learning and achievement. The practices are organized under the strategies of (1) attending to brain fitness and (2) stimulating neural networks. They are only examples of what a leader might do, because, as noted in the Introduction, there are "at least 50 ways" to nurture any dimension of brain capacity. Accordingly, it is intended that the examples offered will stir a leader's further reflection about practices that nurture physiological capacity. The practices presented are also coded by an assessment of their primary (black), secondary (gray), and associated (white) influence on the physiological (P), social (S), emotional (E), constructive (C), reflective (R), or dispositional (D) nature of intelligence.

Practices That Facilitate Brain Fitness

There are innumerable sources that describe activities and programs that nurture mind-body fitness, including literature about aerobic exercise, nutrition, sports, dance, art, music, meditation, and spirituality. The practices that follow are drawn from such resources to describe what a leader might do to promote brain fitness in self and others.

The Practice: PIP.1. Smart Moves

The Place: Smart moves are useful for altering mind and body states in meetings or at work stations. As described here, they can be conducted as simple physical movements that counter the brain-numbing effects of fixed posture and minimal sensory stimulation over extended periods of time.

The Process: Hannaford's 1995 book titled "Smart Moves: Why Learning is Not All in Your Head," is one source that comprehensively examines smart moves that nurture mind and body. A few moves that are appropriate to any environment follow (note: each "move" is a process in itself).

1. Stand and stretch every 30–45 minutes.

2. Alternately conduct portions of the work or meeting from standing and sitting positions.

3. Periodically process portions of meeting content in dyad or triad "cocktail' conversations (i.e., pairs and trios stand and converse further about related meeting content over coffee, tea, juice, or water).

4. Rather than one long session break, provide several shorter restroom and water breaks over the course of the meeting.

5. Stand to high-five and toast great ideas as they happen in the meeting.

6. Establish a "stand as you please" policy by which individuals sit or stand in the meeting as their personal mind and body needs dictate.

7. In larger groups, periodically organize different arrangements of sub-groups for collaborative interaction related to meeting content.

The Payoff: Brain-nurturing blood and oxygen flows with physical move-ment and spurts of social interaction. Planned and structured movement within individual and group work also encourages a disposition to focus on knowledge construction and reflection within prescribed chunks of time.

The Practice: PIP.2. Oxygen Pumps

The Place: Brain-nurturing blood and oxygen flows are induced through simple physical movements and social interactions (as described under PIP.1., "Smart Moves"). The oxygenation and movement of blood is further enhanced, however, by more direct approaches to producing such effect. Several examples follow. The physical space required is implied within each example, but all are appropriate for use by individuals and groups.

The Process:

1. Take a quick break walk. The time for this can be as brief or lengthy as circumstances allow, and the aerobic benefits will be realized accordingly. Even a brisk 5-minute walk up and down the hall, stairs, or block will pump the lungs and move the blood.

2. Breathe deeply. There are any number of ways to do this, but Dennison and Dennison (1994) offer a simple approach in their three-step energizer exercise: (1) Both hands are placed on a desk or table top while sitting and lowering chin to chest to stretch and relax neck and back muscles. (2) While taking a deep breath, the head is lifted up and back to arch the back and expand the rib cage. (3) Slowly exhaling, the head is returned to the chin on chest position and the process is repeated.

3. Go aerobic. This level of oxygenation embraces all of the aerobic options for raising heart rate and increasing oxygen supply over 20 minutes or more of sustained cardiovascular work out. Candidate activities include power walks, hiking, jogging, shadow boxing, lap swimming, bike riding, dancing, tennis, hand ball, or a pick-up game of basketball. Such activities normally require a beginning, mid, or end-of-day time frame and follow-up shower time.

The Payoff: The elevation of blood oxygen generally assists the functioning of the neural system, rendering it more alert and focused. The process of pumping more oxygen into the blood also relaxes muscles and reduces the presence of toxic stress chemicals in mind and body.

The Practice: PIP. 3. Waterworks

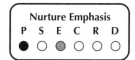

The Place: Given that water is essential to brain composition and operation and that it is continually leaving the body through urination, perspiration, and expiration, it is necessary and appropriate to attend to the hydration of mind and body—anywhere and any time.

The Process: The actual process of hydrating the body could hardly be more simple. Other than in extreme instances requiring intravenous hydration, it is merely a matter of pouring water down the throat. The real challenge then, is not the process itself, but rather the matter of regular and adequate supply over the consumption of diuretics and sugar products that work at odds with water needs. Accordingly, however one might go about it, the essentials of watering the natural waterworks of mind and body involve the following:

1. Ready access to and consumption of water (approximately one 8-ounce glass every two waking hours of the day).

2. Limited consumption of diuretic-laced products such as chocolate, alcohol, and caffeinated coffee, tea, and colas.

The Payoff: Diuretic chemicals in alcohol, coffee, tea, chocolate, and some carbonated beverages cause the body to dehydrate through urination, thus causing constrictions in brain blood vessels, reduction in cerebrospinal fluid, and inhibition of digestive and respiratory processes. When the consumption of such products are limited and the consumption of water is regular and plentiful, the mind and body digest, breathe, oxygenate, and energize to greater effect.

The Practice: PIP.4. Music Moods

The Place: Music is already most everywhere humans venture, including homes, cars, stores, and elevators. Merchants, sports organizations, the military, film directors, and religious groups have long recognized the powerful connection between music and mind-body states. This relationship is instinctual, born of the brain's affinity for patterns as also observed in language, mathematics, and art. Accordingly, music is a useful means to stimulate neural states and relationships appropriate to particular spaces and circumstances.

The Process: The process of music moods is simply one of prompting desirable mind states through music that arouses, subdues, or focuses the brain before, during, or after related activities. Music is also a mind-pleasing accompaniment to transitions between different activities.

The Payoff: Rhythmic patterns in the ear and body connect emotional centers to other neural networks to affect adjustments in mind and body states. Depending on the musical patterns employed, toes tap, bodies move, and thoughts focus—or muscles relax, stress abates, and quiet reflection proceeds.

The Practice: PIP.5. Humor Breaks

The Place: A humor break is an uncomplicated approach to arousing attention, changing posture, relieving tension, provoking thought, and otherwise altering chemical activity in mind and body. It is an activity that can be adapted to any group or location. It is probably best engaged, however, at the beginning or end of defined portions of a group activity (e.g., the beginning or end of a meeting or before or after a meeting break).

The Process: The process of a humor break can be structured many ways, but the basic elements are as follows:

1. Establish value for humor effect on mind, body, and relationships.

2. Establish moral ground rules (i.e., the quality of all stories, jokes, riddles, visuals, etc. must not do harm to any person or group and must be sharable in church or at the family dinner table).

3. Assign a rotation schedule for humor offerings to be presented by specific individuals at prescribed times (impromptu offerings will inevitably emerge once the tradition is established).

The Payoff: The brain appreciates the synaptic jolt it receives from a good laugh and a smile. Laughter is the emotional companion of joy and pleasure. The physical act of laughing enriches blood oxygen while relaxing mind and body. The sharing of humorous stories also promotes social acuity, analytic reflection, and creative and resourceful dispositions.

The Practice: PIP.6. Neural Buffets

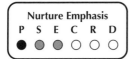

The Place: Healthy food and drink sustain mind-body energy and focus. The foundation of good nutrition rests on established dietary practices within a regular morning, noon, and evening meal schedule. Attention to nutrition can also be advantageously supplemented before, during, between, and after the work activities of individuals and groups. Heavy consumption, however, should be generally avoided, as it takes body energy to unlock energy from food. It is also important to consider the venue and to avoid distractions from tasks or damage to equipment and materials.

The Process:

1. Create and follow nutritious meal plans. This can be approached through vegetarian or nonvegetarian orientations. What is not negotiable, however, is adequate amounts of the basic energy sources of protein, carbohydrates, and fat. A medical advisor is the best source of council regarding the diet that is best for any individual, but the general rules favor water, high protein, complex carbohydrates, and unsaturated fats, with limited intake of salt, sugar, and diuretics such as coffee.

2. Incorporate nutrition in the planning and organization of other materials for individual and group work. With reference to the health food literature, a standard array of nutrition sources can be provided. Water, of course, would always be available. Other options might include apples, pears, bananas, broccoli, celery, carrots, unsalted nuts, yogurt, and whole grain breads and crackers, or yogurt.

3. If nutrition is part of a group activity, rotate planning responsibilities among members to maximize resource variety and knowledge.

The Payoff: We are what we eat and drink, and what we consume will either fire up the energy engines of mind and body or slow them down. Balanced diets provide the materials the brain requires to maintain structures and conduct its information-processing business. Poor diet is associated with stress, depression, and reduced immune systems. Sharing of food in groups, whether at the dinner table or in work settings, is also a time-honored social activity that facilitates information sharing and learning.

The Practice: PIP.7. Touching Moments

The Place: It is human nature to touch and be touched. As a primary means for gathering and processing sensory information, touch is essential to human behavior and learning. Accordingly, touch is necessary and proper within the parameters of appropriate social conduct.

The Process: Touch involves communications between sensory nerves in the skin and muscles that are processed in the sensory and motor cortices and other areas of the brain. A few examples of touching that is helpful to neural health and networking follow:

1. Welcoming handshakes and embraces

2. Affirming pats on the back or touches on the shoulder

3. Celebratory high fives

4. A consoling arm around the shoulders

5. Affectionate hugs and touching of hands

6. Gentle stroking or massaging of shoulders, back, or arm

7. Body massage

8. Water massage (e.g., hot baths, tubs, showers, saunas)

9. Hands-on contact with or manipulation of objects one is learning about

The Payoff: The skin is the largest sensory organ of the human body. To effectively interact and communicate with the world, the brain must make judicious use of this sensory agent. Denied such opportunity, the mind-body is less informed and experiences more stress and depression. Appropriately "in touch" with the world, the brain is more socially informed, emotionally stable, and able to construct useful knowledge.

The Practice: PIP.8. Cohort Aerobics

The Place: Aerobic exercise of various descriptions can be conducted in hallways, stairwells, meeting rooms, parking lots, bike trails, mountain paths, sports fields, aquatic centers, health clubs, or gymnasiums. What

often matters more than the what or where of exercise, however, is who it is shared with. The positive influence of social relationships on commitment, persistence, and achievement is an established phenomenon—one that is embraced by education, business and industry, the military, and most 12-step recovery programs. For that reason, the facilitation of partner and group exercise programs is a worthwhile approach whenever individual and organizational wellness is a goal.

The Process: The process for facilitating cohort aerobics ranges from organizing sign-ups to making arrangements for equipment, sites, and instructors.

The Payoff: To be effective, physical exercise must be engaged according to a prescribed regimen. People who exercise together are more likely to adhere to an elected regimen by virtue of peer support. Thus, physiological mind-body fitness is advanced with valuable by-products of social interaction, stress management, and a disposition to stay the course.

The Practice: PIP.9. Fitness Goals

The Place: It is human nature to establish orienting goals. This is observed at every level of activity, from planting a garden to pursuing a college degree or job promotion. Indeed, the absence of a goal is the best predictor of inaction. If mind-body fitness is to be realized by any individual or organization, then it must be accorded goal status in some fashion.

The Process: It is common practice in most organizations to structure some form of goal planning and assessment. Most often, such structures address both individual and group goals for improved knowledge, skill, and productivity. Accordingly, existing structures will likely accommodate mind-body fitness goals in organizations that value the physiological base upon which improved performance necessarily depends. The process can be as simple as annually setting and assessing mind-body fitness goals (e.g., conditioning, diet, stress reduction) for individuals and groups.

The Payoff: What gets noticed gets attended to. The setting of mind-body fitness goals prompts emotional arousal about what is important to act on for the benefit of the organization and its members. Such action, when associated with organizational goals, also promotes social orientation toward compelling purpose and disposition to plan and organize.

Practices That Promote Neural Networking

Routine and repetitious tasks performed in a consistent environment are not stimulating to neural involvement or development. An environment that is rich in novelty and range of sensory stimulation, on the other hand, encourages greater brain engagement and neural bifurcation—that is, the cultivation of bushy dendrites.

The Practice: PIP.10. Network Alerts

The Place: The brain is a physiological organ that is intimately connected to the body and dependant on sensory stimulation. When lulled into inattention by body fatigue or low sensory input, it benefits from proactive activation of its neural systems. Simple alterations in posture, movement, and breathing provide some assistance to such activation, but additional approaches of more specific design are also available for use in virtually any space and circumstance.

The Process: A time-honored exercise for actively integrating neural networks in both hemispheres of the brain is to pat the top of the head with one hand while rubbing the stomach area in a circular pattern with the other hand—and then reversing rubbing directions and hand locations. Dennison and Dennison (1994) and Hannaford (1995) are sources for other processes that provoke global neural readiness and cooperation in the brain. Two examples follow.

1. The cross crawl is a process of slowly walking in place while touching the knees with the opposite hands or elbows.

2. The hook-up is a process of crossing one ankle over the other while the hands are cross-clasped and inverted (the hands are brought to this arrangement by extending both arms away from the body with

the back of the hands together and thumbs down, then one hand is lifted over the other so that the palms are facing and fingers are interlocked, and then the interlocked hands are rolled down and in toward the body to rest on the chest).

The Payoff: Structured cross lateral body interactions alert neural connections across the corpus callosum and throughout cortical and subcortical brain systems. In this fashion, neural networks are consciously engaged and the brain is focused across its multiple capacities for learning and achieving.

The Practice: PIP.11. Mind-Body Development

Nurture Emphasis
P S E C R D

The Place: There are many established programs that are designed to nurture the intimacy of the mind-body relationship. Given their range and availability, such programs are appropriately accessed when and where individuals and groups wish to engage them.

The Process: The specifics vary greatly, but the general process behind most formal approaches to mind-body development involves conscious reflection about the relationship between the mental and physical self. Examples of such programs that might be of interest to individuals and groups include

1. Weight training/conditioning

2. Marathon training

3. Tae bo

4. T'ai chi

5. Tae kwon do

6. Nai technique

7. Yoga

The Payoff: A very valuable benefit of any mind-body development program is greater understanding of the oneness of human physiology. Such knowledge is constructed emotionally, socially, and reflectively through program participation. Thus informed, a participating mind is neurally disposed to attend to its physiological wellness.

The Practice: PIP.12. Strange Encounters

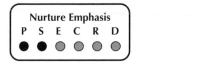

The Place: Anywhere three or more people gather presents an opportunity for presenting the brain with alternate opportunities for novel encounters with diverse ideas and experiences. For that reason, the judicious reconfiguring of groupings when completing tasks or processing or accessing information is a simple but powerful means for stimulating the brain's neural networking. Such organization of alternative brain interactions can be facilitated within in-house meetings, work groups, classrooms, workshops, conferences, and Internet communications.

The Process: Specific practices for arranging and rearranging group configurations (e.g., dyads, triads, base groups, task groups, jigsaw groups) will be presented in Chapter 4. The essence of the process in relation to neural stimulation, however, is that by simply moving brains around within a larger group, a wider range of stimulating encounters with other brains is accommodated. Such movement can be arranged within intimate site-based groups. It can also be accommodated on a global scale by moving people off-site to experience strange encounters with other brains in novel environments in multiple contexts.

The Payoff: The brain feeds on novelty, even when it is frustrating or disconcerting. Variety reduces the brain-numbing effects of encountering the same knowledge in the same way for extended periods of time. Diversity of experience with other brains provokes emotional attention, knowledge construction, reflection, and social disposition. Such encounters pump up existing neural circuits and encourage the construction of new networks.

The Practice: PIP.13. New Ventures

Nurture Emphasis
P S E C R D

The Place: The neural networking of the brain is extended and further interconnected by new environmental experiences. The engagement of information that the brain has not encountered before has the desirable effect of building new neural networks while, at the same time, refining connections to and within existing networks. Thus, ventures that require the mastery of new knowledge and skill are stimulating to neural growth and development.

The Process: The process of embracing new ventures is merely one of periodically exploring a topic, issue, activity, or skill that is unfamiliar, yet of interest to an individual or group. The key is to provide the brain with an environmental encounter that will provoke new learning. Examples of engaging the brain in doing something it has not done before will, of course, vary from individual to individual and group to group. Given that, examples of new ventures for some individuals or groups might involve

1. Learning to play chess, bridge, or other games requiring mental focus and manipulation

2. Learning a new language (fluency is not the issue)

3. Learning a new craft

4. Participation in the arts

5. Exploration of a new field of literature

6. Traveling to experience and study foreign cultures

7. Participation in political debate and/or social activism

8. Participation in a new sport or exercise program

9. Learning about the culinary arts

10. Engaging in some aspect of horticulture (e.g., gardening or landscaping)

The Payoff: Novel experience stimulates the allocation of blood-borne resources to the construction and refinement of neural networks. Through the social, emotional, and reflective engagement of information that is unique to its experience, the brain consciously advances the bifurcation of dendrites and the myelination of axons, thus enhancing its physiological capacity.

The Practice: PIP.14. Thought Walks

The Place: Thought walks offer a simple approach to engaging a productive mind-body connection. This physical exercise of body and brain (favored by the likes of Charles Darwin and Albert Einstein) is applicable to meaningful reflection by individuals and groups anywhere walking space is available.

The Process:

1. Identify a problem, issue, or task that warrants thoughtful attention.

2. Secure pencil or pen and paper for recording thoughts during the walk.

3. Select a walking route that can be covered in the allocated amount of time. Outside routes (e.g., around the neighborhood, hiking paths, a beach area) are the best because of fresh air and multisensory stimulation received from the environment. It is also important that routes be separate or spaced if the activity is conducted with groups.

4. Engage in the walk individually or in pairs or triads and focus on the identified problem, issue, or task using one or more of the following prompts:
   a. How do I/we feel about this?
   b. What do I/we know and what do I/we need to know about this?
   c. What is the preferred/possible outcome?
   d. What is the worse case scenario?
   e. How might someone else (whom I/we respect) approach this?
   f. What is an analogy between this problem, issue, or task and what my/our eyes are observing at this moment?
   g. What are my/our options?

5. At the end of the walk, write down your most important ideas/insights.

The Pay-off: Thought walks get the blood pumping, the oxygen flowing, and neural networks working—networks in the frontal lobes in particular. They are a good two-for-one deal. They employ healthy exercise to physically and kinesthetically support analytic and creative reasoning. Over time, the activity promotes valuable health and thinking habits.

The Practice: PIP.15. Stimulating Space

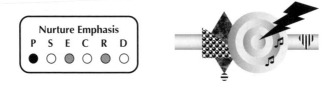

The Place: The neural systems of the brain are turned on by visual, auditory, olfactory, oral, and tactile information. Accordingly, the organization of space configurations and artifacts has unavoidable influence on the brain, wherever it might be or whatever it might be doing.

The Process: The process of providing brain friendly space is generally a matter of accommodating the senses. There is no one recipe for doing this, of course, particularly because the brain likes variety and novelty—and different contexts require different considerations. There is also a wealth of expertise to tap from the field of environmental design regarding this matter. It is always advisable, however, to invite the brains that occupy the space to explore ideas for color, lighting, artwork, furniture, tactile effects, air movement, temperature control, space arrangements, technology, music, sound control, water and other nutrition sources, and the communication of purpose and values. It is also particularly wise to consider the benefits of movable walls and manipulative artifacts that group and provoke brains for different purposes.

The Payoff: Richness of sensory information is essential to the neural networks of the brain. Investments in the quality of space the brain often inhabits are investments in social and emotional orientation, information sources for knowledge constructions, and productive habits of mind.

Reader Reflection

With reference to the preceding story, this section provides an opportunity for reflection about the related knowledge constructions that are occurring in your brain about the nature and nurture of physiological capacity. To that end, the template that follows this section will facilitate your reflective response to three questions:

1. What do you now know about the physiological nature of intelligence?

2. What does this knowledge mean to you (i.e., what are the most important insights, conclusions, or implications that emerge from what you know)?

3. What action(s) will you pursue given what you know and judge to be important?

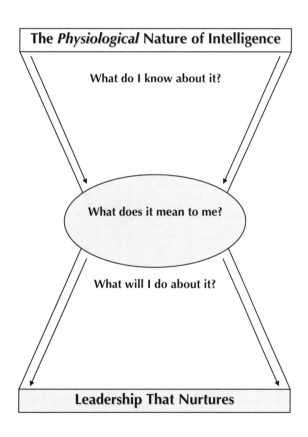

4

Social Nature and Nurture

The Story of Social Capacity

Evelyn's brain is an uncompromising social extrovert. It is profoundly disposed to hang out and interact with other brains. The behind-the-scenes story of this very social brain is that it is designed by nature to attend to the activities and products of other brains. Evelyn's brain both expects and depends on the provocation of social experience to do its job well. This social expectation and dependency is characteristic of all humans. Indeed, the strength of this social bias has motivated the brain to invent ways to reach out and connect with more brains.

Behind the Scenes

For as long as we have been around as humans, as wondering bands of nomads or cave dwellers, we have sat together and shared experiences. We have painted images on rock walls, recounted dreams and visions, told stories of the day, and generally felt comforted to be in the world together. When the world became fearsome, we came together. When the world called us to explore its edges, we journeyed together. Whatever we did, we did it together.

—Wheatley (2002, p. 4)

Evelyn's big brain is big on relationships. This is so, in part, because her brain is a product of nature's propensity to organize relationships between elements. This disposition to organize parts into systems is observed throughout the universe, from the organization of electron, proton, and neutron particles into atoms to the organization of planets and stars into solar systems and galaxies. Evelyn's brain, then, is an example of nature's capacity for organizing biological relationships. As described in Chapter 2, her brain is a complex system of highly interactive relationships among cells, circuits, and chemicals. Indeed, Evelyn's brain is the most complex system on Earth.

Evelyn's brain is also strongly oriented to relationships because of its social heritage. Born of rich social experience over many millions of years, her brain is endowed with hyper-social instincts—natural and powerful abilities for memory, language, empathy, sympathy, collaboration, and reasoning.

Consider the social circumstances of Evelyn's early ancestors and what such existence would provide, require, and reward. Those social communities sought survival advantage from cooperative efforts in surveillance, food gathering, and problem solving. Such cooperation and proximity encouraged capacity for memory of individuals, events, relationships, geographical markers, and food sources. Infinite opportunities to observe what others were doing also encouraged mimicking of behavior and associative learning. There was also opportunity and need to be attuned to other members of a group if one was to take advantage of warnings or other important information. This attention encouraged refined sensory processing of visual and auditory information aligned to body and verbal signals. Thus, language emerged within the intimacy of social communities.

Social proximity also placed a premium on being attuned to the mind and body states of others and the opportunities and dangers therein. Attention to such matters eventually contributed to a socially acquired sense of empathy and sympathy for others. This was pivotal to the development of conscious reflection in the brains of Evelyn's ancestors. It was a development that encouraged acuity in recognizing and communicating a wide range of emotional experience. It also laid the emotional groundwork for moral and artistic reflection. The neural ability to perceive what another was experiencing also prompted reasoning operations involved in calculation, imagination, and moral judgment.

Behind the scenes, then, the evolution of Evelyn's brain has benefited greatly from a long history of social influence. You might say that her brain is both relationship composed and disposed.

Great Expectations

Evelyn is heir to a brain forged in social experience. The product of that evolutionary experience is a brain that is aware of itself and incredibly adept at observing people and events, remembering important information, learning from others, communicating visually and verbally, exercising emotional awareness and judgment, and reasoning reflectively. Notably, this capacity born of social experience remains loyal to its origins.

Evelyn's brain expects to encounter and interact with other brains. Deprived of such opportunity—particularly in youth—its potential for exercising memory, learning, language, emotion, and reasoning is greatly diminished. The proof of this social expectation in the extreme is observed in situations of abuse and autism that prohibit human interaction. In such instances, a brain is denied the means to unfold its genetic program of neural circuitry and master the fundamentals of sense of self, language, and moral orientation. Evelyn's expectations for instructive social interaction go beyond the basics, however, to learning the nuances of human culture such as body language, intuition, attentive listening, conscious observation, and artistic expression.

The bottom line is that Evelyn's brain is brought on line and up to speed by its encounters with other brains. It is a brain that expects to establish interactive cellular relationships within itself through interactive relationships with brains outside of itself.

Depending on Others

The developmental unfolding of Evelyn's brain requires interactive relationships with the environment, particularly interpersonal relationships, to realize its potential. That is, "human connections shape the neural connections from which the mind emerges" (Siegel, 1999, p. 2). Evelyn's brain is thus experience expectant in the process of sculpting essential neural networks. Evelyn's brain is also experience dependant, however, in that it relies on a quantity and quality of environmental experience to continually expand and refine its neural capacity. What is a matter of development in youth is also a matter of refinement and maintenance throughout life. Interaction with other brains continues to be a primary means for exercising and refining intellectual capacities. The knowledge and ideas of others are engaged through observation, conversation, dialogue, debate, reading, writing, and artistic representations. Such interaction continually stimulates emotional attention, pattern recognition, cognitive dissonance, and reflective reasoning. It physically influences electrochemical activity that directs neural network growth and rewiring. It is how Evelyn is provoked to ponder, question, and explore—and continually grow in knowledge and wisdom.

Social experience, then, is the great provocateur of thinking and learning. Evelyn's brain depends on such provocation to continue to grow and do its best work. Indeed, this dependency is so great that Evelyn will go to great lengths to access it.

Reaching Out

Social experience is what Evelyn's brain expects and depends on, no less than lungs depend on oxygen and eyes require light to do their work. Fortunately for Evelyn, this need is nurtured by technologies that enable brains to interact with each other when they are physically separated.

Over sixty thousand years ago, brains of limited language capacity began to communicate graphically through cave paintings. Fifty-some thousand years later, other more verbally adept brains created the symbol systems that enabled the first forms of written language. By these developments, human communication moved beyond direct face-to-face interaction to an expanded society of minds—a society that included the recorded knowledge of brains that were distant in space and time.

The inventions of art and written language were followed by other initiatives to enhance the scale and quality of human interaction. This is demonstrated in the communication technologies of printing, photography, radio, cinema, television, and, more recently, the Internet. Such communication vehicles have been augmented by transportation technologies and a wide variety of art forms that further expand the means by which Evelyn gains access to other minds.

This urge to reach out to other brains arises from the survival mission of Evelyn's brain. There is safety and survival in social membership. That survival advantage is served particularly well by interactions that network the collective knowledge of many people, whether they are present, distant, or deceased. The product of such networking is clearly evident in every instance of significant human achievement. Great accomplishments in any field of human endeavor are never the products of lone genius. The contributions of individuals are to be noted, but no mind is untainted by the minds of others. A lunar landing, medical breakthrough, or exceptional work of art are all accomplishments of a human society of mind. Who could or would profess an absence of neural bridging to the ideas and experiences of others?

The Meaning of the Story

> One of the things that marks humanity out from other species, and accounts for our ecological success, is our collection of hyper-social instincts.

> —Ridley (1996, p. 6)

Despite whatever appearances to the contrary, Evelyn's brain is social to the extreme. Granted, Evelyn might at times affect shy or withdrawn behavior, but not likely to the exclusion of all interaction with other minds in the media forms of books, newspapers, magazines, radio, television, telephones, or the Internet. The social nature of Evelyn's capacity to think, learn, and achieve is simply commanding. It both requires and facilitates interaction with other brains. Denied such opportunity, Evelyn's brain will not unfold according to its genetic program, nor will it perform to its potential. Operating Evelyn's brain without social experience is like operating a flashlight without batteries.

What, then, is the bottom line, the meaning of all of this for leadership? What qualities of Evelyn's social brain are particularly worth understanding and nurturing? Perhaps, it is suggested here, a leader might be mindful that Evelyn's capacity to learn and achieve is socially hyper, expectant, dependant, extended, and virtuous.

Hyper

Born of rich social experience over millions of years, the human brain is endowed with hyper-social instincts—natural and powerful abilities for memory, language, empathy, sympathy, collaboration, and reasoning. The brain's social instincts are constantly engaged through the senses of sight, hearing, taste, smell, and touch. Evelyn directly reads, watches, listens, ingests, inhales, moves, feels, and touches to gather information from the environment. At more refined levels, moreover, Evelyn observes an expression, detects a pattern of behavior, reads between the lines, notes the inflection, hears what is not said, feels the tension, smells the excitement, tastes the fear, and otherwise detects nuances that richly inform understanding and reasoning.

Expectant

The unfolding of brain capacity to think, learn, and achieve is expectant of the same social experience that constructed it. Social interaction is a critical attribute of environmental information experienced by Evelyn's brain. It is a primary means by which Evelyn's neural circuitry is activated and reinforced.

Dependant

Social experience is the great provocateur of thinking and learning. Beyond fulfilling Evelyn's expectations for social experience, interpersonal relationships are the foils by which Evelyn's neural networks are productively maintained and refined. Thus, Evelyn's capacity to think, learn, and achieve profits immeasurably from quality associations with provocative people, ideas, and events.

Extended

To satisfy its overarching need and disposition to interact in a society of mind, the human brain has invented a variety of media that extend social interaction beyond face-to-face encounters. Whether direct or indirect, social interaction engages a flow of energy and information through a collective human intelligence. It is through interpersonal neural networking on a grand scale, moreover, that the best ideas are generated, critiqued, and refined—and collective human potential to think and learn is realized in the process. It is such networking that both generates and disseminates art, philosophy, and moral perspective. Most important, communities of mind emerge from such networking to solve difficult problems, create better systems, and invent new technologies.

Virtuous

The brain has an instinctive moral orientation to prosocial behavior. The human measure of what is right and what is wrong arises from millions of years of species evolution in a social context. The golden rule is neither chance observation nor the exclusive property of world religions that universally embrace it. Evelyn's moral perception of what is good and what is bad reaches back to the social origins of humanity. What Evelyn would like to happen to Evelyn is the bottom line measure of what is socially good and just for all—to be safe, sheltered, fed, loved, and free. Evelyn may not always act in accordance with this perception, but Evelyn's brain always knows whether Evelyn's behavior is in line with what is fundamentally right and wrong.

The Rest of the Story

Evelyn's story up to this point is the tale of a hyper-social animal, an extrovert who has high social expectations and needs and will go to great lengths to satisfy them. The story that remains to be told, however, is what might happen to Evelyn in reality contexts. Just because nature has endowed Evelyn with an extraordinary social capacity to acquire and apply knowledge does not mean that such capacity will be appropriately nurtured in home, school, or place of work. Following, then, is the rest of the story—what might be done to counter the capacity-sapping conventions of cubicles, desks, and stations.

Mindful Strategy

Given that social capacity is important to how Evelyn naturally thinks, learns, and achieves, it is important for a leader to be mindful of strategies for nurturing such capacity in individuals and groups. Three examples follow.

Strategy: Facilitate Meetings of Minds

When one brain meets another brain, the exercise of thinking and learning inevitably follows. This is why two or more heads are literally better than one in socially adept collaborative groups. Accordingly, a leader might contemplate ways to facilitate the organization of cohorts, teams, and other groups as appropriate to specific responsibilities and tasks.

Strategy: Cultivate Common Purpose

Making a contribution to the common good is what counts to the social orientation of the brain. The collective capacity of human intelligence is tapped when the brains within an organization are enticed into collaborative relationships by clear, compelling, and mutually held goals. Accordingly, a leader might consider ways to facilitate dialogue about vision and purpose and action and progress.

Strategy: Extend the Mind's Reach

The strongest ropes are woven from diverse fibers. Diversity of experience and perspective in social interactions enhance the prospects for productive thinking and learning. This is particularly important to resolving challenging problems and tasks. Accordingly, a leader will promote diversity of background in task groups, access to distant brains through media, and on-site and off-site professional growth experiences.

Mindful Practice

This story concludes with a description of practices a leader might employ to nurture the nature of Evelyn's social capacity for learning and achievement. Continuing the schema presented in Chapter 2, the practices are aligned to the previously offered strategies of (1) facilitating meetings of minds, (2) cultivating common purpose, and (3) extending the mind's reach. The practices presented are also coded by an assessment of their primary (black), secondary (gray), and associated (white) influence on the physiological (P), social (S), emotional (E), constructive (C), reflective (R), or dispositional (D) nature of intelligence. Once again, the practices offered are only examples intended to prime a leader's reflection about what he or she might do, because there must be at least 50 ways to nurture the social dimension of brain capacity.

Practices That Facilitate Meetings of Minds

An obvious approach to facilitating productive interactions between brains is to reference the extensive knowledge base about collaborative learning. A leader who understands the principles underlying effective group collaboration thereby gains access to a vast array of formats for facilitating the social exercise of intelligence. Slavin (1990), Kagan (1992), and Johnson and Johnson (1999 and 2002) are but a few of many rich sources for practical, research-referenced implementation formats.

The Practice: SIP.1. Brain Wave

The Place: The most direct and uncomplicated approach to accessing the social intelligence of a group is to structure a spontaneous outpouring of information and ideas. As will be suggested through the array of practices described in this and other chapters, there are innumerable ways in which this can be done. A brain wave, however, is a simple and ready-to-use process that can be adapted to any context that values the immediate attention and involvement of all brains present.

The Process: The social dynamic of a brain wave can be pictured as the succession of sea waves breaking on a beach or the classic wave produced by sports spectators sequentially standing and extending their arms around the parameter of a stadium. The idea is just that, to sequentially bring forth the collective resources of a society of minds in rapid, sequential order. It is an activity that is particularly useful for initiating social dialogue in larger groups but is applicable to smaller assemblies as well. The process, in its many adaptations, is basically as follows:

1. A facilitator directs a question or issue to the group.

2. Members of the group are then asked to offer information, questions, observations, or ideas in response to the prompt in a very brief, sequential fashion. This might be structured by moving from person to person in a clockwise direction around a table or (with a larger group) moving progressively from one side of the room to the other with volunteered responses at the direction of the facilitator (and perhaps repeated in successive "waves").

3. Following this initial engagement of social intelligence, the next steps depend on the meeting purpose (e.g., discernment of common themes, questions, or knowledge in the wave(s) of responses; formal presentation of relevant content; or further sharing and analysis of related information in various social groupings).

The Payoff: The brain is emotionally invited to knowledge construction and reflection by a social process that encourages the universal participation of all brains present. The brain wave process also promotes the dispositions of listening, questioning, and being open to information and ideas.

The Practice: SIP.2. Dyad Processing

The Place: Little is more common to human experience than to turn to another person and share the contents of one's mind. Not only is this natural behavior, it is also essential to how the brain learns. It is fortunate, then, that dyad processing of understanding, ideas, and questions can be accommodated anywhere and anytime two or more people are present—even when their presence is electronic in nature.

The Process: Structured applications of dyad processing can be modified and adapted in many different ways to accommodate content and context, but the basic process is as follows:

1. Periodically pause within a presentation or large group discussion so that participants can assimilate their processing of content.

2. Participants select a partner (someone sitting in close proximity is a time and convenience consideration) and briefly (e.g., 2–3 minutes) reflect and share their understanding, observations, or questions related to relevant content.

3. If there is more than one dyad involved, the larger group briefly (e.g., 2–3 minutes) processes insights or questions that emerged from the pair groups and then continues the original presentation or discussion.

The Payoff: Dyad processing is the simplest and most direct means to socially integrate the resources of multiple brains. Intimate social interaction accesses sensory information that emotionally arouses neural networks to the work of constructing and reflectively manipulating knowledge. Social interaction also promotes the dispositions to listen, reflect, and collaborate.

The Practice: SIP. 3. Triad Processing

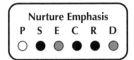

The Place: Triad processing of information and tasks serves the brain in the same fashion that dyad processing does. If two heads are better than one, moreover, the addition of a third amplifies the dynamic of one thought building upon another. The obvious advantage is increased diversity of knowledge and skill in the grouping. Triads are applicable to all contexts in which three or more people are gathered and good thinking is desired.

The Process: As in the case of the dyad process, structured applications of a triad process can be modified and adapted in many different ways to accommodate content and context. The basic process is as follows:

1. Periodically pause within a presentation or discussion in a larger group so that participants can assimilate their processing of content.

2. Direct participants to organize a triad (individuals sitting in close proximity is a time and convenience consideration, but random groupings will produce more diversity of thinking over time) and briefly (e.g., 3–5 minutes) reflect and share their understanding, observations, or questions related to presentation content.

3. If there is more than one triad involved, the whole group briefly (e.g. 3–5 minutes) processes insights or questions that emerge from the triads and then continues the large group presentation or discussion.

The Payoff: The triad process is a somewhat more sophisticated means to socially integrate the resources of multiple brains. Intimate social interaction accesses rich sensory information to emotionally arouse neural networks to the work of constructing and reflectively manipulating knowledge. Compared to a dyad process, the triad process also places a slightly higher dispositional premium on the productive habits of listening, reflecting, and collaborating.

The Practice: SIP.4. Progressive Processing

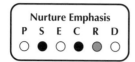

The Place: If two heads are better than one and three better yet, one might logically conclude that thinking will be further enhanced by the involvement of even more brains. This, of course, is close to the heart of *Leading With the Brain in Mind*—to cultivate a collective organizational capacity for learning and achievement. The idea that the more brains the better only holds, however, to the degree to which groups are effectively structured. Fortunately, there are a variety of such structures available for organizing the progressive processing of information in groups larger than three.

The Process: The general idea behind the progressive processing of information is to move from the exercise of individual intelligence to the exercise of collective intelligence. A common approach is progressive movement from the individual to small group to (when appropriate) large group. For example, in a group of 24, the process might be organized as follows:

1. Identification of a topic or question to be addressed.

2. Division of the group of 24 into 6 groups of 4 (by random selection, such as counting off by 6, to generate diversity within subgroups).

3. Arrangement of the small groups in a manner that facilitates face-to-face interaction (e.g., around a table or a circle of chairs).

4. Selection of a manager in each group for time management and reminding the group of their task and procedural rules.

5. One member of the group shares information and ideas related to the assigned topic within a time limit (e.g., 1–2 minutes) while other members listen and take notes but do not interrupt or ask questions.

6. The other members share information, observations, and ideas in the same fashion in a clockwise order.

7. After all members of the group have shared their initial thoughts, a second round might be conducted for generating further information.

8. The group engages in dialogue to pursue key insights, themes, and questions that emerged from the individual sharing.

9. A debriefing is conducted to share small-group insights, themes, and questions with the large group.

10. The large group identifies common and unique insights, themes, and questions across the debriefing of the six subgroups.

The Payoff: Individual brains construct understanding of important topics and issues through productive social interactions with other brains. Progressive processing, in its many forms and adaptations, structures access to the constructive and reflective resources of many brains in an efficient and orderly fashion. It is a practice that emotionally arouses and focuses the brain while promoting the productive thinking dispositions of listening, analyzing, and synthesizing.

The Practice: SIP.5. Basic Jigsaw

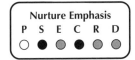

The Place: Jigsaws structure the collaborative learning of divisible information (e.g., the contents of books, chapters, reports, or conceptual models) in groups.

The Process: Anchored by extensive research and diverse models (e.g., Sharan & Sharan, 1976; Aronson, Stephan, Sikes, & Snapp, 1978; Slavin, 1990, Johnson & Johnson, 1999), jigsaws are structured many ways (e.g., see a progressive version in Chapter 6). The essence of the process, however, is relatively simple and can be conducted by as few as two people:

Organization of Subgroups

The larger group is divided into subgroups (e.g., one to six members) and each subgroup is assigned a specific portion (i.e., piece) of the targeted content

Task Assignment
1. Construct personal understanding of assigned content.
2. Explain/teach content to others.

Preparation in Subgroups
1. Individually review assigned material to identify key content and ideas.
2. Reach group consensus about main ideas and other key content.
3. Design a strategy for explaining/teaching assigned content to others.
4. Prepare visuals and handout material.

Presentation and Processing in Large Group
1. Subgroup explanation/teaching of assigned content to large group within allotted time and with attention to
   a. Related information sources
   b. Implications of assigned content for related content and issue
   c. Active learning involvement by the audience
2. Whole-group question-and-answer discussions following presentations

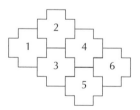

The Payoff: The jigsaw process engages the brain's bias for constructing knowledge through direct social interaction. It progressively promotes emotional attention, knowledge construction, and reflective decision making, as well as the dispositions to listen, question, be creative, cooperate, and plan well.

The Practice: SIP.6. Corner Conversations

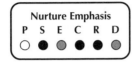

The Place: This activity originates from the common human practice of congregating in small groups on street corners or in areas of a room to converse about matters of concern. It is used to explore a topic or issue in a manner that encourages sharing of information, analysis, debate, and discovery. Depending on the size and number of groups, space is required for groups to congregate in a prescribed number of corners (e.g., 2–5 or more). Corner groups can range in size (e.g., 3–15), but smaller is generally better.

The Process:

1. Clarify the topic or issue to be explored.

2. Determine the dimensions of the topic or issue to be discussed in corners. This step can be focused in any manner that serves the purpose of the activity. It can be as simple as having the large group divide into smaller groups to converse about how they feel and what they know and want to know about a particular topic or issue. Another approach would be to jigsaw the analysis and summation of a portion of a topic or issue in smaller groups. Yet another approach is to organize participants into different exploratory groups focused on multiple positions or questions related to a topic or issue (e.g., pro or con positions, questions about what is known or unknown, causes, resources, possibilities, problems, facts, alternatives, comparisons, projections, or explanations).

3. Identify conversation corners in the room or other environmental space and assign conversation groups to corners as determined in step two.

4. Allow adequate time for productive corner discussions. Depending on how the corner conversations are structured, groups might also be reconfigured or moved clockwise or to opposite corners to further promote progressive processing of information.

5. Reform as a large group and debrief and discuss what was learned, questioned, or decided in the corner conversations.

The Payoff: Corner conversations encourage divergent and convergent thinking around a topic or issue of interest. Social sharing of information and perspectives engages emotional attention to the construction of knowledge, as well as reflective decision making and problem solving. Such conversations also promote the dispositions to listen, question, seek clarity, and be creative.

Practices That Cultivate Common Purpose

Practices that influence a sense of common purpose will range in complexity and sophistication (and will therefore be further addressed in Chapter 6). The general idea, however, is to afford involved brains the opportunity to reflect together and find motivational agreement about what is important to do and how to go about doing it.

The Practice: SIP.7. Inspirations

The Place: The brain has an instinctive social orientation to issues of welfare and achievement. For that reason, the brain is emotionally focused by inspirational readings or other accounts or depictions of commitment to compelling purpose. Such inspiration can be drawn from literature, art, historical reference, current events, personal experience, or other sources. It is also easily adaptable to individuals and groups in any time and place.

The Process: Inspirational readings or stories or other references can be incorporated into the work of individuals and groups in many ways, but a direct and easily managed approach would be as follows:

1. Reflect upon the value of inspiration to the work of the individual and/or group.

2. Establish sources of inspiration (e.g., from literature, art, history, philosophy, biography, current events, personal experience).

3. If conducted individually, establish a regular time and place for inspirational reflection (e.g., beginning of the day, midday, end of day, or combinations thereof).

4. If conducted in a group, assign inspiration responsibilities to members on a rotating schedule (e.g., at the beginning and/or end of meetings).

The Payoff: Born of social experience, the brain is instinctively focused by issues of human welfare and achievement. Stories and other depictions of human commitment and accomplishment promote emotional arousal and conscious reflection about human purpose in relation to the work immediately at hand.

The Practice: SIP.8. Before and After Action Reviews (BAAR)

The Place: It is natural for human groups to gather and orient themselves to their collective work both prior to and after embarking on particular tasks and responsibilities. This is observed in schools, hospitals, police and fire departments, military operations, and sport events. Accordingly, the BAAR practice is applicable to a variety of group sizes (e.g., the members of a department or an entire organization) on diverse schedules (e.g., daily, weekly, monthly, quarterly, or by event).

The Process: Whether demonstrated in the form of a morning tea, day-report, huddle, or Pueblo kiva, the essence of a BAAR process is

Before
1. Gathering of group members in one location (this can be done electronically)
2. Reference to a guiding mission or purpose
3. Discussion and agreement about what will happen in a given time period or event

After

4. Gathering of group members in one location (physically or electronically)

5. Discussion of the events and results that occurred within the given time period and what adjustments should be made in the future

The Payoff: BAARs structure social and emotional commitment to compelling purpose. This orientation focuses physiological, constructive, and reflective intelligence resources on defined goals. BAAR also promotes collaborative, analytic, and creative thinking.

The Practice: SIP.9. Base Groups

The Place: Consistent with the systems orientation of the universe, it is the nature of humans to organize themselves into systems within systems. Thus, the family is the fundamental group from which individuals further organize into extended families, neighborhoods, communities, businesses, institutions, states, nations, and international organizations. As systems become large and complex, however, the individual brain remains dependant on intimate and sustained affiliations with other brains. Such relationships help the brain maintain clarity about what is most important to do and how to do it. A base group of three to six members, then, is a practical means for providing social support for goal achievement in any context.

The Process: Base groups can be organized in many configurations and formats, but the general process involves dividing the larger membership into subgroups of three to six members by natural affinities within the organization (e.g., members of the same department or division). Once established, the purpose of the base group is to provide dialogue and support for its members through regularly scheduled

1. Peer reviews of goals and goal progress (both individual goals and related organizational goals)

2. Peer reviews of the requirements of specific tasks and assignments

3. Peer reviews of progress on specific tasks and assignments

4. Peer assistance in knowledge acquisition and skill development

5. Peer assistance in problem solving and conflict resolution

6. Peer awareness and support for the life events affecting members outside of the organizational environment

The Payoff: It is the business of the brain to survive and thrive. This natural inclination benefits from structured social interactions that orient and support goal achievement within larger systems. Peer support in base groups is particularly helpful to the management of emotional stress, the construction of knowledge, reflective planning and problem solving, and the cultivation of a collaborative and empathetic disposition.

The Practice: SIP.10. Action Planning Groups

The Place: Action planning groups share some characteristics of base groups but are distinct in their social engagement of what, when, where, why, and how decisions about common goals. They are also a means for focusing group resources within an efficient meeting format. A tightly scripted action planning process is useful in any context requiring collective expertise, action, and assessment of progress toward an agreed purpose.

The Process: There are various formats for conducting planning groups (e.g., see additional and more comprehensive formats described in Chapter 6). A key consideration, however, is to structure the process in a manner that focuses the energy and expertise of the group in an efficient and effective manner. The following example is an adaptation of Schmoker's (1999) format for productive and time-efficient (i.e., 30 minute) meetings.

Before the Meeting
1. Prepare and distribute an agenda so that members arrive aware of the focus and schedule and ready to contribute ideas and information.
2. Assign management tasks (e.g., a facilitator, recorder, timekeeper).
3. Prepare necessary materials (e.g., writing materials, markers, flip chart, information sources).

During the Meeting

4. Quickly reference the issue or problem to be addressed (1 minute).
5. Discuss previous challenges and successes regarding the issue or problem (3 minutes).
6. Discuss current concerns related to the issue or problem (5 minutes).
7. Brainstorm potential solutions to a primary concern related to the issue or problem (10 minutes).
8. Write an action plan for implementing the most promising solution generated and supported by the group (10 minutes). The plan should include a very concise (i.e., one page) description of (a) the issue or problem, (b) the proposed action, (c) the measurable objective of the proposed action, (d) data that will be gathered to assess the result of the proposed action as measured by its stated objective, (e) a timeline for conducting the action, and (f) who will conduct and manage the plan.
9. Schedule the next meeting (1 minute).

After the Meeting

10. Communicate meeting minutes and copies of the action plan.

The Payoff: The brain emotionally commits to goals it understands and values. Social participation in action planning promotes the construction of knowledge from shared information, reflective problem solving, and the dispositions to cooperate, listen, analyze, create, plan, and assess.

Practices That Extend the Reach of the Mind

The brain benefits immeasurably from direct social interaction with other brains. The advantage of pooling neural capacity is further compounded when such interactions are extended to brains beyond physical presence.

The Practice: SIP.11. Book Groups

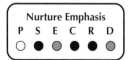

The Place: Book groups offer a relatively easy way to build a collective knowledge base. They also extend the mind's reach to the rich information sources of brains beyond the immediate context. Book groups can be facilitated in almost any location, but membership will ideally be diverse in order to promote multiple perspectives and lively debate and interpretation.

The Process: Book groups can be organized in multiple ways, but the general elements of the process might be assembled as follows:

1. Select a book that offers rich text related to a valued focus (e.g., leadership, learning, attributes of successful organizations).

2. Decide how the book will be read (e.g., jigsaw by chapters, chapter a week read by all, sections read with guiding questions in mind).

3. Develop a timeline for reading and meeting.

4. Select a facilitator among group members to ensure lively discussions that are highly engaging for all participants.

5. Determine what follow-up applications are appropriate to the purpose of the reading (e.g., general reflection and refinement of knowledge or application to a task at hand).

6. Solicit proposals and determine the next book to be read.

The Payoff: Bringing together a diverse group of people to read and discuss a good book expands their society of mind to include brains they might not otherwise engage. It is a process that emotionally excites and physically stretches their brains in the process of constructing and refining knowledge. The social processing of rich reading material also promotes the productive dispositions of listening, questioning, analyzing, and synthesizing.

The Practice: SIP.12. Mentor Relationships

The Place: A mentor is a wise and trusted teacher or counselor. Accordingly, mentoring assumes a relationship between a novice and an expert. It is a process that represents an opportunity to extend the mind's reach beyond relationships with brains that one might normally hang out with. Whether one is the mentor or the mentee, the relationship automatically presents a disparity of knowledge and experience—the qualities of dissonance and novelty that the brain depends on for learning. The mentoring process, then, is applicable and of benefit in any situation where there is need and availability of expertise. It is also a process that can be one-on-one or adapted to groups of various sizes.

The Process: A mentor relationship is a sustained association in which the teacher or counselor provides support and guidance that helps the novice grow in knowledge, skill, and character. The mentor has two critical roles. One is that of an expert and the other is that of a role model. The structuring and conduct of a mentoring process can be and is organized in many ways. The simple and time-honored tradition of conversation over a cup of coffee or other beverage probably works as well as any other format. In essence, nevertheless, it is a process that involves

1. Introduction and biographical sharing between mentor and mentee

2. Agreement about the mentoring focus, content, and procedures

3. A schedule for interactive sharing of information through dialogue, observation, shadowing, modeling, and feedback

4. Periodic assessment and celebration of the relationship

The Payoff: The greater the diversity of experience and perspective in social interactions, the greater the prospects of constructing new knowledge and meaningful reflection. Mentoring relations facilitate the skill and knowledge acquisition and problem solving associated with new ventures. It also helps manage emotional stress associated with novel challenges and promotes the disposition to be organized, reflective, and proactive. It is also important to note that all of those benefits accrue to the brain of the mentor as well as the mentee.

The Practice: SIP.13. Professional Affiliation

The Place: Active membership in professional associations extends the mind's reach to distant peers, advancements in the field, and structured and unstructured opportunities for learning. Association affiliations can be productive at local, state, national, and international levels.

The Process: There is no definitive process for professional affiliation. The basic idea is to join and hang out with an association of other brains that are active in your field of expertise and share your professional interests. Just joining up and paying dues, however, is not the idea behind this practice. To fully appreciate the advantages of a professional affiliation, a leader will

1. Access periodicals and other media published by the association

2. Compose and submit articles for publication in association media

3. Participate in association institutes, conferences, and workshops

4. Prepare and submit proposals for presentations at association institutes, conferences, and workshops

5. Participate in social events connected with association institutes, conferences, and workshops

6. Report and otherwise share information from association media, institutes, conferences, and workshops with colleagues

7. Network with interesting brains encountered at association events

The Payoff: The proactive engagement of professional affiliations is a classic approach to securing novel and enriching social encounters. It is a means to connect with expertise and experience that is exceptional to one's normal context. It is an opportunity to affiliate with the "best" and most active brains within a given field. Such association is emotionally and socially supportive of ongoing knowledge construction and reflection. It also promotes an essential professional disposition toward continual learning and openness to new information and ideas.

The Practice: SIP.14. Alien Alliances

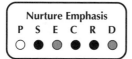

The Place: An alien alliance is a process that pursues professional growth through social interaction(s) with individuals who have expertise and experience outside of one's normal context. It is a valuable approach to provoking the brain to construct and refine knowledge through novel encounters with unfamiliar information and perspectives. It can be conducted in pairs or groups in any context that can accommodate interactions between brains of diverse background and expertise.

The Process: The basic idea behind an alien alliance is to expand one's worldview through structured interactions with individuals who can provide unfamiliar—but useful—information and perspective. Such interaction can be organized as simply as conversation over a cup of tea or on the Internet. It can also be formatted as progressive encounters between members of larger groups. In any case, the essential steps include

1. Interaction between individuals from different organizations, fields, cultures, or of other discriminating description (e.g., business, education, medicine, government, gender, age, nationality) that will assure diversity of expertise and experience

2. Focusing of the interaction by sharing of personal experience and perspective related to a specific topic (e.g., leadership, management, education, economics, the arts, resolution of a particular problem)

The Payoff: The greater the diversity of experience and perspective in social interactions, the greater the prospect of strong productive thinking. A brain is emotionally provoked to think new thoughts and construct new understanding from encounters with brains that offer different information and interpretations. Thus, experiences with alien alliances are important to cultivating the dispositions to be open minded, adventurous, and analytic.

The Practice: SIP.15. Technology Adventure

The Place: At the beginning of the twenty-first century, a human mind can literally reach out to interact with other minds anywhere at anytime. To not take advantage of such ability, then, is to miss a great opportunity to participate in the ever expanding society of mind—across both the globe and the span of time.

The Process: The process involved in a technology connection, obviously, is specific to the technology one is connecting to. Accordingly, the description of process offered here will not encompass that detail, but will point to the options one has to tune in and turn on to the resources of other brains. Such options range from the tried and true to the very new:

1. Read books and articles (i.e., the printing press remains a power-house technology in bridging the thoughts of brains across time and space).

2. Listen to books and articles via disks and tapes.

3. Listen to a variety of radio stations when traveling or engaged in activities that allow productive listening. Music is always a good choice for physical and emotional effect and reflective ambiance, but to get the social, emotional, constructive, reflective networks firing, one will access National Public Radio and talk shows (whether of a con-servative or liberal slant; they will stimulate your neural connections in any case).

4. Mix it up on television as well. Cable and satellite systems assure that there is always something of a rich information nature available to feed to your brain (one must avoid the brain-numbing content, but the history, literature, debate, philosophy, geography, travel, science, comedy, and arts programming is there to be taken advantage of).

5. Television is also beginning to come into play more commonly in interactive distance learning.

6. Film and video options are getting better due to an increased presence of independent and international productions in the market.

7. The Internet has no limits in its reach to content and dialogue.

The Payoff: With limited effort, accessing technology extends the reach of the mind to the rich sources of brains removed in time and space. Such access facilitates emotional engagement, knowledge construction, reflection, and a general disposition to exercise and nurture the mind.

Reader Reflection

With reference to the preceding story, this section provides the opportunity for reflection about the related knowledge constructions that are occurring in your brain about the nature and nurture of social capacity. To that end, the template that follows will facilitate a reflective response to three questions:

1. What do you now know about the social nature of intelligence?

2. What does this knowledge mean to you (i.e., what are the most important insights, conclusions, or implications that emerge from what you know)?

3. What action(s) will you pursue given what you know and judge to be important?

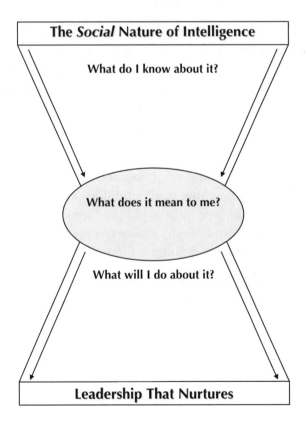

5

Emotional Nature and Nurture

The Story of Emotional Capacity

The story of Arnold's brain is an emotional one. It is a story about how the brain is aroused to do its work—a matter of movement in mind-body states associated with attention, judgment, and motivation. It is also an account of the important relationship between emotion and reflective reasoning in the brain.

Emotion, You Move Me

Emotions are complicated collections of patterned chemical and neural responses that regulate an organism in a manner that is advantageous to its survival.

—Damasio (1999, p. 51)

Arnold is moved by emotion because emotion arouses adjustments in his mind and body. Most important, the process of emotional arousal provides him with an essential survival edge, an edge that strongly orients advantageous action both prior to and during thoughtful reflection. As Siegel (1999, p. 124) has described it, "Emotional processing prepares the brain and the rest of the body for action."

Emotion is a survival mechanism that evolved in life forms that needed to efficiently screen, judge, and react to a vast array of environmental information. It is a collection of quick response systems that have been highly refined in humans by rich social experience and high mobility over a long period of evolutionary time. Beyond arousing initial responses, it is also a means for focusing subsequent reflection and action. Emotion is a process, then, like digestion or respiration, rather than a thing, like a heart or kidney. It involves biological processes that regulate Arnold's mind and body responses to subjective evaluations of internal and external information.

Notably, Arnold's emotional processing of information from stimulus to action is much more automatic and efficient than his cognitive processing of information from stimulus to action. Just as Arnold's brain has circuits that unconsciously regulate his autonomic system's operation of basic body survival activities (like breathing and blood circulation), it also has subconscious neural circuits that subjectively screen information for patterns that swiftly arouse prescribed mind-body responses. Arnold is only made aware of the activation of such emotional processes when he feels the transitions they have triggered in his mind and body. Thus aware, he can then consciously reflect about how he might best proceed given what has already transpired.

Arnold is particularly moved by the primary emotions of fear, anger, happiness, sadness, surprise, and disgust—emotions that are universally observed across all cultures (Ekman, 1984). He is also influenced by the many variations of primary emotions such as the anxiety, concern, or nervousness associated with degrees of fear or the pride, rapture, or whimsy associated with happiness. Regardless of the nuance, however, the range of emotional processes available to Arnold collectively attend to both the basic and subtle requirements of human survival.

Before You Know It

The emotional nature of Arnold's brain dictates an "act first, think later" response to information. Accordingly, emotion is very much in the driver's seat in determining what Arnold will attend to and how he will initially respond to what captures his attention. The basic process is as follows:

1. Neural networks in various regions of Arnold's brain (e.g., in the amygdala and brain stem) comprise "emotion centers" that regulate mind and body responses to particular configurations of internal and external information. Those neural centers operate as sentries that monitor information brought forth for their inspection through the brain stem, thalamus, and olfactory lobe.

2. Upon detecting an information pattern judged to be of importance to its particular responsibilities (e.g., information suggesting danger or opportunity), an emotional center will inform other parts of Arnold's brain about its discovery and concern.

3. Thus alerted, related neural networks initiate prescribed transitions in mind and body states through neural synapses and chemical releases into the blood stream that enable actions judged to be in Arnold's interest (e.g., to fight, flee, or focus).

4. Subsequently, other neural networks become aware of the transitions that are occurring in Arnold's mind and body—they *feel* the emotional response.

5. Finally, Arnold's prefrontal cortex and other cortical areas are informed by feelings related to emotional events. After his subconscious brain has reflexively reacted, Arnold is presented with the opportunity to consciously reflect about what is happening and what more he might want to do about it.

This ready-fire-aim arrangement between the reflexive and reflective qualities of Arnold's brain is, again, born of its evolutionary heritage. Emotion is an older, faster brain-body mechanism for processing and responding to environmental information. Accordingly, Arnold's emotional centers screen and make decisions about information entering the brain before his reflective centers are involved. That is, emotion happens, literally, before Arnold knows it. This is a necessary relationship for two reasons. First, in cases of extreme threats to survival, emotional reflex is much more efficient than reflective thought. If a an object is unexpectedly moving rapidly toward his head, Arnold benefits from ducking first and reflecting later. In such instances, his reflective capacities are placed on hold as his brain is emotionally hijacked to take care of first things first (LeDoux, 1996). Second, as capable as Arnold's brain is, it cannot attend to everything, and the emotional screening of any and all information advises his reflective brain about what is worth thinking about. Thus, this attend-react-then-think approach is at work in all aspects of Arnold's life experience—be they large or small, dramatic or mundane.

When You Know It

Arnold is often very aware of emotion-charged states in his body and mind as they happen. For example he is likely aware of changes in mind and body when a red light flashes in the rearview mirror of his car, a fire alarm goes off, someone invites him to dance, the phone rings in the middle of the night, or he wins the lottery jackpot. In instances when more subtle emotional processes are at play, Arnold's awareness of what is happening in his subconscious brain is less dramatic. There is a point, however, where the escalation of emotional arousal activates conscious feelings, what Damasio (1999) refers to as the "feeling of what happens." This brain capacity for consciously "feeling" transitions in body states is thought to have been a critical factor in the evolution of an awareness of self and, thereby, the capacity for conscious reflection and construction of knowledge.

There is an important distinction to be made between emotion and feeling, two words that are sometimes uses synonymously. A feeling is generated by emotion and is something that Arnold becomes aware of and can do something about. Emotion, on the other hand, will do what emotion will do, and Arnold will not be aware of it until its work becomes manifest in the form of a feeling. What is important about this is that upon becoming aware of a feeling (i.e., "when you know it") a brain can then consciously review its options.

Emotion moves Arnold to attention, judgment, and motivation. It initially involves neural and glandular systems that trigger immediate responses to evaluations of external and internal information. Subsequently, however, emotional centers interact with rational reasoning systems in his brain to further judge the merits of events and available options. Emotion also plays a role in motivation by sustaining Arnold's attention to things that matter. Accordingly, emotion becomes manageable after the fact of its initial effect. Arnold is able to recognize and mediate emotion as it evolves. The degree to which he is able to do so defines his "emotional intelligence"—what Salovey and Mayer (1990), Goleman (1995, 1998), and others generally describe as the ability to manage emotion in a manner that contributes to the quality of life.

Beyond the basic arousal function of emotion in mind and body, then, is the nature of its relationship to the complex thinking capacities of Arnold's brain. Conscious awareness of an emotional effect is the gateway to reflection about how to manage the power of emotion to advantage. As Sylwester (2000) described it, sensory information patterns activate emotional systems, which activate brain attention and, most importantly, capacity to construct understanding, solve problems, and make decisions. In this fashion, emotion is in partnership with Arnold's cortex not to resolve, but to involve. From systems located primarily in the lower and older areas of his brain, emotion initiates a process that informs his prefrontal cortex as to what it should be thinking about. Arnold's cortex, in response, acts to understand what has been brought to its attention and to generate behaviors that will relieve related concerns.

Still a Player

Emotion is an old and proven survival system that is still very much in charge of human behavior. Indeed, as Pert (1997) observed, there was a chemical nervous system in the body that employed molecules of emotion before there was a central nervous system that incorporated emotion in its electrochemical communications. This is an important point. As the brain evolved and assumed its system management and decision-making responsibilities, it incorporated the body's existing communication system. Thus, Arnold's brain informs and affects his body, and his body informs and affects his brain. He truly does have a mind-body. This "two-way street" arrangement is observed when Arnold's nervous stomach trips emotional centers in his brain and when emotional alerts in his brain initiate physical responses in his stomach.

The point is that emotion is still very much a player in how Arnold thinks and behaves. As much as he or anyone else might like to think he is capable of a purely rational approach to life, the scientific fact is that his mind and body are awash with emotion. There is literally nothing that Arnold thinks about or does that is not accompanied by emotional markers. Accordingly, it is advisable that he and his associates acknowledge the character and influence of his emotional being. For example, the primary job of emotion is to alert other systems about the need for their services. Upon detecting an information pattern of concern, emotional networks adopt an energy consuming posture—they literally light up with the electrochemical flow of information to arouse transitions in mind and body. A problem arises, then, when Arnold's emotional networks are over engaged. It is equivalent to running a car engine at top speed for a sustained period of time; such stress damages components of the system. Neural networks are subject to damage from the extended presence of chemicals such as the cortosol secretions involved in a fear response. Along the same lines, intense or sustained surges of emotion "highjack" Arnold's brain to a basic survival focus. In such instances, his access to analytic and creative-thinking services in his prefrontal cortex is compromised. Emotionally overwhelmed, he finds it difficult to attend, learn, remember, or make decisions. As Goleman (1995, p. 149) suggested, "Stress makes people stupid."

Another emotion matter that warrants attention is that more neural communications flow from emotion systems to complex reasoning systems in Arnold's brain than from complex reasoning systems to emotion systems. The good news about this arrangement is that Arnold is responsive to meaningful challenges that both require and sharpen his reflective problem-solving and decision-making capacities. The predominant directional flow of information from emotion to reflection also provides Arnold's "thinking" cortex with opportunities to refine its emotional intelligence, that is, to manage emotion in a manner that contributes to his welfare and quality of life.

Most important, emotion does not dance alone on the multidimensional stage of Arnold's intelligence. Emotion exerts a strong influence on his brain's physiological fitness, social acuity, knowledge construction, reflective reasoning, and thinking dispositions. Thus emotion interacts intimately with the other major players involved in Arnold's capacity for learning and achievement.

The Meaning of the Story

Arnold is aroused in mind and body by his emotional brain to do what it takes to survive and thrive. Absent this emotional dimension, he would be literally unable to determine where to go or what to do. A leader must decide, then, what leadership consideration should be given to this quality of intelligence. A determination must be made about the meaning of Arnold's story—what is most important to know and do regarding the emotional capacities of self and others. To that end, knowing how Arnold's brain is emotionally attentive, judgmental, motivated, and manageable might be particularly worthy of leadership attention and action.

Attentive

Emotion involves neural and glandular systems that trigger changes in mind-body states—reflexive changes that arouse brain attention to what is important.

Arnold's brain is emotionally attentive. The resources of his mind and body are aroused and focused by emotional assessments of what merits attention. Accordingly, his brain will not easily attend to what is perceived to be insignificant or inconsequential. Arnold's brain will also find it difficult to attend to matters that are important if it is emotionally distracted by concerns for its immediate physical or social welfare.

Judgmental

Reflexive arousal systems associated with emotion interact with rational reasoning systems in the brain to evaluate the merits of events and options. Arnold's brain is emotionally judgmental. It is constantly weighing the advantages and disadvantages of every situation. Although much of this occurs at a subconscious level, it extends to Arnold's reflective capacities, as he cannot make reasoned judgments without emotional input. All of his efforts to rationally analyze, solve, decide, and resolve are performed in concert with emotional assessments of what is best to do.

Motivated

Emotion both arouses and sustains passion about things that matter. Arnold's brain is emotionally motivated. Beyond an initial assessment that something is worthy of attention, the continuing allocation of mind-body resources depends on ongoing dialogue between his emotional and reflective brain centers about the value of the issue or task at hand.

Manageable

The brain is able to recognize and mediate emotional responses—a capacity referred to as emotional intelligence. Arnold's emotional brain is manageable to the degree that Arnold is adept at regulating emotional effects. The power of emotion must be managed to informational and motivational advantage by the rational capacity of the brain. Done well, regulation of emotional states enhances the quality of Arnold's life.

The Rest of the Story

> *No doubt humankind's original leaders—whether tribal chieftains or shamanesses—earned their place in large part because their leadership was emotionally compelling.*

> —Goleman, Boyatzis, and McKee (2002, p. 5)

Arnold's story tells the tale of a brain that is emotionally attentive, judgmental, and motivated—and manageable only to the degree that conscious reflection is invited to the party. Thus emotion is cast as the gatekeeper that directs the involvement of other dimensions of intelligence. Emotion is a major player on the stage, and simply expecting self and others to be "rational" isn't going to cut it. Arnold is going to be emotional under any and all circumstances. Indeed, he is *always* emotional before he is aware of a need to be rational. The rest of the story, then, is one of harnessing the power of emotion.

Mindful Strategy

Given that Arnold's brain is aroused and focused by emotion, a leader will advisedly consider ways to establish a productive alliance with the powerful forces that move mind and body. Three suggested strategies for doing so follow.

Strategy: Ease the Mind

The brain will not attend to other tasks if it is emotionally distracted by concerns for its physical or social welfare. It is important, therefore, for a leader to consider means by which the brain can be made to feel safe, valued, and supported.

Strategy: Excite the Mind

The resources of the brain are aroused and focused by emotional assessment of what merits attention. For that reason, it is advisable that a leader seek to orient the brain to matters of compelling value, vision, and purpose.

Strategy: Evaluate States of Mind

The power of emotion must be managed to informational and motivational advantage by the rational capacity of the brain. Accordingly, a leader is encouraged to facilitate reflection about emotional states and the means to regulate and manage such states to maximum advantage.

Mindful Practice

Arnold's story concludes with descriptions of practices a leader might employ to nurture the nature of emotional influences on learning and achievement. Continuing the schema presented in prior chapters, the practices are aligned to previously offered strategies: (1) ease the mind, (2) excite the mind, and (3) evaluate states of mind. The practices presented are also coded by an assessment of their primary (black), secondary (gray), and associated (white) influence on the physiological (P), social (S), emotional (E), constructive (C), reflective (R), or dispositional (D) nature of intelligence. Once again, the practices are only examples intended to prime a leader's reflection about the 50 or more ways that he or she might nurture the emotional nature of the brain.

Practices That Ease the Mind

Many practices that support brain fitness, such as those involving movement, music, and humor, have a valuable collateral effect on the management of emotional stress. This fitness effect on emotion demonstrates the mind-body connection as described in Chapter 2. There are many other practices that promote the brain's emotional composure, however, as represented by the following examples.

The Practice: EIP.1. Group Norms

The Place: The establishment and referencing of group norms or ground rules is a practice that structures professional and productive social interaction in the work place. Norms or rules provide guidelines for how the group will function with an eye to maximizing group effectiveness and efficiency, while minimizing confusion, disruptions, and conflicts. Accordingly, the establishment of norms is a process that is best initiated early in a group formation stage. It can be also be adapted and employed, however, in any context and circumstance that will benefit from a respectful and comfortable emotional climate.

The Process: The establishment of group norms is essentially a process of coming to agreement about the way members of a group will interact with each other when conducting their common business. One approach to establishing such norms is as follows:

1. Begin with a discussion of the stages of development that any team goes through. For example, individuals form a group, storm about

their business in somewhat awkward fashion, norm their interactions with each other from experience and habit, and – if all goes well – begin to perform as a team. This developmental process might also be described as the grouping, groping, growing, and grasping model. The point to be made is that groups naturally progress through stages as they mature and become high performing.

2. Extend the discussion to the consideration of the need for norms to encourage productive behaviors leading to a high functioning team. This discussion might benefit from a worse case/best case scenario reflection around the topic of forming a new group.

3. Define group norms as guidelines for how members will know what is expected of them.

4. Form pairs or triads for brainstorming two or three essential norms (worded affirmatively) for the group to consider (e.g., to listen attentively to one another, start on time and end on time, critique ideas – not people, stay on task, be patient with each other, no put downs, work only on things that cannot be best accomplished by memo).

5. Share small-group suggestions and consolidate similar ideas.

6. Allow time for reflection about suggested norms because they will become rules to live by. After such reflection, facilitate consensus at a later meeting about the norms that will adopted by the group (note: it is best to limit the number of norms to three to six).

7. Post the norms and/or review them briefly prior to each meeting.

8. Be flexible and realistic. Think of norms as general guidelines, not rigid laws.

9. During the last 3–5 minutes of each meeting evaluate how effective the group was in adhering to its norms and how it might improve the next time it meets.

10. All teams violate their norms on occasion. If a norm is repeatedly abused, the group needs to decide whether or not it is a problem. If it is, consider giving feedback to the abuser(s) or discussing the issue as a group—or change or drop the norm.

The Payoff: Group norms provide structure and clarity for human interaction. By establishing clear and positive professional expectations for behavior, the brains in the group experience greater emotional safety and confidence. Norms help groups avoid the physical stress that occurs when confusion, disruption, and conflicts impede the work of a group. Established norms of behavior can also improve the effectiveness and efficiency of the group's social interactions. That, in turn, facilitates a collective capacity for analysis and creativity, as well as a range of productive dispositions that evolve from effective collaborations.

The Practice: EIP.2. Peer Interviews

The Place: Peer interviews are useful for managing emotional stress when members of a group do not know much about each other or when new people join an established group. It is a process that is easily organized in any context.

The Process: The process associated with peer interviews can be modified in multiple ways, but the general approach is to have participants interview other people to obtain and report information. Hence, the practice might look like this:

1. The focus for the interview is determined (e.g., to obtain biographical information, and/or information about professional interests and accomplishments, and/or information about an interesting life experience from the interviewee).

2. The logistics of the interview are determined (e.g., group members will interview each other in pairs, or each group member will interview at least three other members of the group, or each new member of the group will be interviewed by two veteran members of the group).

3. The interviews are conducted and notes recorded within a prescribed time frame (e.g., 5–30 minutes).

4. Interview findings are reported to the whole group. This is conducted in a manner aligned to the interview logistics (e.g., if the interviews were conducted in pairs, the pairs might introduce each other to the group. If the process involved multiple interviews or interviews of new members, an individual might be asked to stand and his or her interviewers would then take turns sharing information about that person).

The Payoff: The peer interview process confronts the issue of social-emotional awkwardness and anxiety head-on (i.e., "brain-on"). The process structures social interactions that promote emotional comfort, attention, and motivation. It also paves the way for collaborative knowledge construction and reflection as members of a group are relieved of the distractions of emotional distress or uncertainty. The more a group is aware of the talents of others, the more disposed it might be to risk the provocative social interactions the brain requires to do its best work.

The Practice: EIP. 3. Member Checks

The Place: Member checks acknowledge and accommodate the emotional influences at work among the members of a group. As such, the process affirms that the brain is always emotional first, and then reflective. It is a process of emotional assessment and release. In engaging in the process at the beginning and/or end of any meeting or learning session, participants share (i.e., unload) the emotional influences on their mind-body states.

The Process: A member check process can be organized as either a fixed or periodic practice to be conducted in groups that meet regularly. As a routine for checking in at the beginning of a meeting, it might be simply organized by one or two of a selection of questions as follows:

1. What interesting, exciting, or challenging things have happened in the world since the last time we met?

2. What interesting, exciting, or challenging things have happened to members of this group since the last time we met?

3. What questions need to be answered in our meeting today?

4. What concerns do you have about the direction we are headed?

5. How are you feeling about being here?

6. Are there any feelings or past events or practices that are preventing us from moving forward and collaborating effectively?

Similarly, at the end of a meeting the group might address one or two questions that assess the emotional dimensions of the work at hand:

1. How are you feeling as you leave here today?

2. What are we doing well?

3. What do we need to do differently the next time we meet?

4. What are you looking forward to doing/experiencing between now and the next time we meet?

The Payoff: The brain is always conducting emotional assessments of any climate or task it encounters. Accordingly, quick member checks are means to set participants at emotional ease and create social readiness to learn and be fully engaged in the work of the group. Such checks invite concerns, questions, and other emotional distractions to be voiced and heard. They also promote the dispositions of being empathetic, focused, and clear.

The Practice: EIP.4. Victory Laps

The Place: The victory lap process is a practice that facilitates an emotional orientation to what is going well and is right with the world. It can be conducted in small, medium, or large groups in any context calling for reduction of emotional stress and promotion of positive perspectives.

The Process: This is one of those incredibly simple yet important practices that can be exercised quickly and often. The most basic and direct way to conduct it is to have members in a group volunteer or progressively share (e.g., clockwise around a table) something that is going well, a recent proud moment, a success story, or some other such victory in life's journey.

The Payoff: It is important that people share what is going well. A victory lap facilitates that sharing. It is an approach to flushing the mind and body of neurotransmitters and hormones associated with stressed and depressed states. Thus emotionally relieved and reoriented, the brain is less distracted from its knowledge construction and reflection tasks. It is also more disposed to be positive and proactive.

The Practice: EIP.5. Positive Affirmations

The Place: Positive affirmation provides emotional release and orientation. It is a practice that can be conducted individually and in groups anytime there is advantage to be gained from a positive perspective about what is possible.

The Process: The heart of the process of positive affirmation is accenting the positive. It is a process, of course, that can be, and is, formatted to many different contexts. The example that follows is adapted from one described by Vaughan (2000, p. 157) in her account of the positive outlook advantage realized by subjects who focused on "I'm glad I'm not . . ." sentence completions as opposed to "I wish I were . . ." sentence completions.

1. Identify a sentence stem that will focus reflection about positive advantage (e.g., I'm glad that . . . , An advantage we enjoy is . . . , An opportunity within this situation is . . .).

2. Individually complete the sentence stem with different endings a minimum of five times.

3. If conducting the practice as a group, share and compile the sentence endings.

The Payoff: The brain can think its way to a positive state of mind and optimism by the exercise of its reflective capacity for projecting options and alternatives. This is an example of the brain applying what Schwartz and Begley (2002) refer to as "mental force." That is, the brain realizes the emotional welfare and disposition of optimism by doing what an optimist does.

Practices That Excite the Mind

There is a strong tie between emotion and social experience. Social encounters are naturally exciting to the brain. The brain is turned on and provoked by social experience. In fact, it expects and depends on such interaction. Accordingly, all of the practices described in Chapter 3 (i.e., facilitating meetings of minds, cultivating common purpose, and extending the mind's reach) have an associated effect on emotional arousal. Indeed, an important purpose of structuring social encounters and orientations is to emotionally arouse the brain to attention and commitment. Following are additional practices for exciting the mind.

The Practice: EIP.6. Anticipatory Set

The Place: An anticipatory set is a process for capturing and focusing the brain's attention. It can be conducted with any size group in any context when people are shifting mental gears from one activity to another.

The Process: As the name suggests, the purpose of an anticipatory set is to create some condition of intrigue that will cause the brain to anticipate what it is going to happen next. Popularized by Hunter (1982), it is a process that elicits attending behavior (i.e., deliberate focus) and a mental readiness or "set" for the content of an ensuing activity. Accordingly, an anticipatory set should only continue long enough to get the brain focused and ready to engage the objective(s) of the task at hand. There is also ample room for fun and drama in anticipatory sets, but the basic idea is to start with a mental bang that grabs the brain's attention. A few classic examples follow:

- Ask a focusing question that individuals briefly think about or write an answer to and then discuss with a partner.
- Present a provocative reading, video clip, or recording related to the content or task to be addressed.
- Conduct a brief role-play that addresses elements of the content or task at hand.
- Have participants briefly talk in pairs about what will be learned or accomplished in their time together.
- Review the major issues, concerns, or accomplishments of the prior meeting or task.

The Payoff: The resources of the brain are emotionally aroused and focused by ongoing judgments about what merits attention. An effective anticipatory set overtly invites the brain's attention to worthy content and tasks. The outcome is a brain that is engaged and ready to learn and achieve. A byproduct is a disposition to clarify purpose and focus on tasks.

The Practice: EIP.7. Mission Set

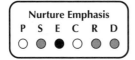

The Place: A mission set is useful when participants in a meeting or task need to answer to the question, "why are we here?" A reference to the organizational mission provides a mental orientation or "set" that aligns the task at hand to a compelling purpose. It is a practice that evokes emotional attention, judgment, and motivation by referencing a guiding statement of important common purpose. A mission set is particularly appropriate when planning, problem solving, or making decisions.

The Process: The mission set process assumes an organizational mission statement that it is familiar to all participants (or in view as a posting or handout). Given that ready reference, the process is a matter of answering questions:

At the beginning of a task or meeting:
1. What is our mission?
2. What is the task at hand (e.g., project, problem, decision)?
3. How does this matter serve or challenge our mission?

At the end of the task or meeting:
4. How did our efforts today advance our mission?

The Payoff: The referencing of the mission of the organization solicits emotional and social alignment to a compelling purpose. Such alignment encourages related knowledge construction, reflection, and collaborative disposition.

The Practice: EIP.8. Personal Set

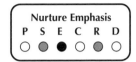

The Place: A personal set is a practice that references personal values and experience to evoke emotional attention, judgment, and motivation about a task at hand. It is a process that can be conducted individually or in groups anytime it is desirable to help the brain become more emotionally engaged and productive.

The Process: The process of conducting a personal set is primarily one of assessing personal priorities and past, present, and future relationships. Thus the steps in the process might be organized as follows:

1. What is the task at hand (e.g., project, problem, decision)?
2. What is my past experience with the task at hand?
3. How does the task at hand relate to my personal beliefs and values?
4. How is the task at hand connected to my current priorities?
5. How will I be involved with the task at hand today and in the future?

The Payoff: The referencing of personal values and experiences solicits emotional alignment to a compelling purpose and personal sense of mission. Such alignment encourages related knowledge construction and reflection. When conducted and shared in a group, it also solicits social alignment to common purpose and collaborative dispositions.

The Practice: EIP.9. Reality Set

The Place: Referencing a reality context provides a mental orientation or set that evokes emotional attention, judgment, and motivation related to the big picture. It is a practice that can be conducted individually or in groups anytime it is desirable to help the brain see relationship(s) between immediate concerns and other and greater contexts and purposes.

The Process: The process of conducting a reality set is primarily one of assessing the relevance of specific tasks and concerns to a greater context or purpose. One approach might be to ask some or all of the following questions at the beginning of a meeting or initiative:

1. What are major events or issues challenging the world/this organization today?
2. What is our current task/focus (e.g., project, problem, decision)?
3. What is the connection between major events and issues confronting the world/this organization and the task/focus at hand?
4. How will world events and issues affect our current task/focus?
5. How will our current task/focus affect world events and issues?
6. How will our current task/focus affect everyday events and issues?
7. How will our current task/focus affect our clients?
8. How will our current task/focus affect the people in this room?
9. Why is this task/focus worth our time and effort?

The Payoff: A reality set aspires to emotionally excite the resources of the brain through conscious reflection about what merits attention and why. Whether conducted in classrooms or boardrooms, such arousal to emotional assessment is a means to perceive the need to focus knowledge construction and reflectively solve problems and make decisions. Conversely, it is also a means to promote the dispositions to seek clarity and question the effective allocation of mental resources.

The Practice: EIP.10. Future Set

Nurture Emphasis
P S E C R D

The Place: A future set commonly references current, possible, and preferred states. It is a planning tool for establishing a mental set through reflection about where programs, individuals, or groups are and want to be. It is a practice that invites emotional attention and judgment about matters of great motivational consequence to participants. It is a process that can be used for individual reflection and planning, but it is usually conducted in small groups of three to six at tables supplied with paper and marking materials.

The Process: There are many formats for reflecting about the future (e.g., as described in other practices in Chapter 6) and, thereby, soliciting emotional assessment and commitment. The following is one approach:

1. If working with a larger group, divide participants into work groups of three to six (randomly select to promote diversity of experience and ideas).

2. Have each group select a facilitator to manage participation, procedures, time, and recording of information.

3. Identify the subject of the future prospects assessment (e.g., a program, an event, an individual, a group, or organization).

4. Provide a model of the following graphic process for participants to replicate on paper or newsprint in their planning group:

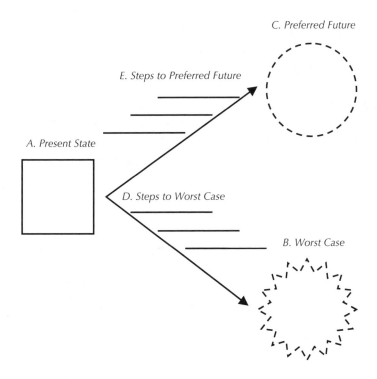

5. Beginning with *A. Present State*, have subgroups brainstorm and record the present state of the subject (i.e., "the good, the bad, and the ugly"). Subgroups then report their assessment to the large group.

6. Proceed to *B. Worst Case*, and have the subgroup discuss and record the future characteristics of the subject if everything that could go wrong did (and again share their conclusions with the large group).

7. Have subgroups then turn their attention to *C. Preferred Future* to forecast the desirable attributes and conditions that would describe the subject if everything good that could happen did (and again share their conclusions with the large group).

8. As a whole group, identify and post common elements from subgroup descriptions of the present state, worst case, and preferred future.

9. With reference to the agreed upon elements of worst and preferred state scenarios, have the subgroups brainstorm and record steps (i.e., actions) on the lines provided that would move the subject toward *B. Worst Case* or toward the *C. Preferred Future*. (Note: It is important that the groups identify *D. Steps to Worst Case* before they contemplate and describe *E. Steps to Preferred Future*.)

10. Have subgroups share their assessments of influential steps to the worst case and then steps to the preferred future. As a whole group, then identify common steps from among the reports.

11. Using nominal group process techniques, conduct a whole-group prioritization of essential steps (i.e., actions) necessary to realize the preferred future—and recruit volunteers to begin that work.

The Payoff: A conscious orientation to the probable and possible future solicits emotional concern and motivation. The involved social processing pools knowledge, as well as collective reflection about options. The practice also promotes proactive dispositions toward change, planning, and collaboration.

Practices That Evaluate States of Mind

Emotions move mind-body states in response to environmental stimuli prior to conscious reflection. Upon feeling the effects of emotion in mind and body, however, the brain can assess the states that are unfolding and what might best be done to manage what has already occurred. Such evaluation and management of emotion to advantage is a matter of emotional intelligence—the reflective regulation of emotion in a manner that contributes to the quality of life.

The Practice: EIP.11. Emotion Check

Nurture Emphasis
P   S   E   C   R   D

The Place: An emotion check is the practice of emotional intelligence on the fly. It involves efficient awareness and management of emotional movement in mind and body in a manner that contributes some degree of survival advantage. It is a practice that is incidental to the motion of emotion as it happens, but strengthened by continuous applications in all contexts. It is particularly useful in highly stressful, depressing, or stimulating environments. Most often exercised by the individual brain, assessments of emotional motion and response are also useful in groups.

The Process: The process of an emotion check is simply one of consciously reflecting about the emotional state of one's mind and body and what to do about it. That is, it is a process of asking, "What am I feeling and how might I manage that feeling to my further advantage?" In some cases, the motion of emotion is clearly revealed to the conscious brain due to intensity of effect (e.g., fear or exhilaration). At other times, however, the workings of emotion might be subtler (e.g., low-level stress over time, a nagging anxiety). In the latter instances, a proactive assessment of what emotion is in motion is required. The process, then, is basically one of asking a few questions and then acting according to the answers. For example,

1. What am I feeling (e.g., anger, joy, frustration, confusion)?

2. Why am I feeling it (e.g., someone cut me off in traffic, I received an important promotion, I cannot adequately communicate my idea, I'm not clear about what they expect)?

3. What would be a good thing to do about what I am feeling (e.g., take a deep breath and count to ten, be modest and reserved in my success, try to present it another way, ask for clarification).

The Payoff: Emotion is the gatekeeper to other intelligence capacities of the brain. If not managed well after the fact of being triggered in mind and body, it can direct behavior in a detrimental direction (e.g., road rage, debilitating sadness, loss of focus). Efficiency in recognizing and managing emotion, on the other hand, is a means to enhance the social interaction and reflective reasoning important to planning, problem solving, decision making, and conflict resolution. And, of course, a disposition to monitor and manage the motion of emotion is a desirable habit of mind.

The Practice: EIP.12. Mood Check

The Place: Sylwester (2000) advises that emotion is the weather of the moment, while mood is a weather front that moves through and lingers for hours or days. A mood check, then, is the practice of emotional intelligence at a deeper level than an emotion check. It involves awareness and management of sustained emotional movements in mind and body. It is a practice that is applicable to all contexts but particularly useful in situations where there is stress or an abundance or dearth of environmental stimulation over a period of time. Most often exercised by the individual brain, assessments of emotional mood and advantageous responses are also useful in groups.

The Process: The process of a mood check is one of consciously observing a sustained emotional state of mind and body and what to do about it. It is a process of asking, "What is my emotional mood and how might I manage that mood to my advantage?" In some cases, the mood one is experiencing is clearly revealed to the conscious brain due to an intensity of effect (e.g., sadness, anger, or exuberance that hangs on for hours of days). At other times, however, the workings of emotional mood might be subtler (e.g., listlessness, a slight elevation of nervous energy). In the latter instances, a proactive assessment of mood is required. The process, then, is basically one of asking a few questions and then acting according to the answers. For example,

1. What kind of mood am I in (e.g., angry, anxious, enthusiastic)?

2. Why am I in this mood (e.g., I'm still bothered by what happened last night, I'm worried that we won't finish this project on time, things have been coming together and there are good prospects for success)?

3. What would be a good way to go about changing or sustaining the mood I am in (e.g., lighten up, take a break, exercise, go to a movie, read a book, spend time with friends, confront the real issue, continue to accent the positive, anticipate challenges and roadblocks)?

The Payoff: Managing emotional moods need not be rocket science (the caution here, of course, is to differentiate common mood states from serious mental health concerns such as clinical depression). The influence of mood on individual and group capacity must be recognized and attended to, however, if potential for learning and achievement is to be realized. The investment of time in simple mood state reflections and actions offers the return of less distress and distraction in the brain as it attends to its business of constructing and manipulating knowledge. The physiology of the brain also benefits from the proactive reduction of stress-related chemicals (e.g., cortisol) in the brain. Thus, again, the disposition to monitor and manage the motion of emotion in mind and body is a productive habit of mind.

The Practice: EIP.13. Climate Check

The Place: Climate describes the prevailing atmospheric qualities, the weather if you will, of a geographic area. A climate check, then, is an approach to assessing the atmospheric qualities of an organization. More specifically, it bridges the practice of emotional intelligence to discriminating qualities of organizational culture and planning. It is a useful practice in groups and organizations in all contexts when the goal is to emotionally assess and commit to criteria associated with effective organizational cultures.

The Process: The climate check process engages members of a group in identifying and acting on critical attributes of organizational culture that affect productivity and success. As variously organized in different formats, the practice progressively processes reflection from individuals to subgroups to the whole group. An example of how the steps might be executed follows, as adapted from Sapher and King (1985):

1. Divide the group into subgroups of three to six and provide descriptions of attributes associated with successful organizational cultures, for example, attributes described by Peters and Waterman (1982), Lezzote (1997), Cunningham and Gresso (1993), and Collins (2001). After reading the descriptions, subgroups share observations and ask questions to clarify understanding of the various attributes.

2. Provide each subgroup with multiple copies of the following worksheet with a listing of the described attributes of effective cultures in the first column (e.g., collegiality, experimentation, high expectations, trust and support, appreciation and recognition, caring, celebration and humor, inclusive decision making, tradition and ritual, open communication). Have each member of the subgroup circle the two or three attributes they consider to be most important to a successful organizational culture. Then have the subgroups share their selections, reach consensus about the two or three most important attributes, and report their selections and rationale to the whole group.

1	2	3	4	5	6	7
Attribute	Current State	Preferred State	What Detracts	What Supports	What Can Be Done	What I/We Will Do
1.						
2.						
3.						
4.						
5.						
6.						
7.						

3. Process whole-group consensus about the two or three most important attributes of a successful organizational culture and have members of every subgroup highlight those attributes on their worksheets.

4. Have individuals record their reflections in Columns 2–5 about
   a. The current state of the highlighted attributes in their organization
   b. The preferred state of highlighted attributes in their organization
   c. Factors that detract from highlighted attributes in the organization
   d. Factors that support highlighted attributes in their organization

5. Have subgroups share reflections about columns 2–5, reach agreement about common themes, and report conclusions to the whole group.

6. As a whole group, process common themes from subgroup reports regarding Columns 2–5.

7. With reference to whole-group themes about the current and preferred status and factors that detract from or support important attributes of successful cultures, have subgroups use Column 6 to brainstorm and record specific actions that would move the highlighted attributes toward the preferred status described in Column 3.

8. Following reports of recommended actions from subgroups, reach whole-group consensus about one or two actions that hold the greatest promise for favorably influencing each of the targeted attributes.

9. With reference to Column 6 whole-group consensus, have each member commit to developing and implementing the action they personally believe will have the greatest influence on one of the targeted attributes that is important to their organizational culture.

The Payoff: A successful organizational culture begins with an emotional appeal to the rational brain about what makes a difference to the achievement of important purpose. In assessing organizational climate, the brains of the organization are aroused to evaluate and act on emotional commitment to aligned social interaction, problem solving, and disposition to collaborate.

The Practice: EIP.14. Parking Lot Meeting

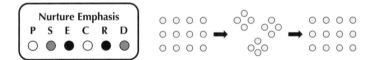

The Place: Impromptu meetings often take place in parking lots and other locations after the formal meeting ends—particularly when the formal meeting does not go well. This activity brings such informal gatherings "inside" to make them part of the formal meeting. It is an activity that can be employed with any group in any context. Its purpose is to have participants share what they perceive has happened during a meeting and how they feel about it. It is an activity designed to build trust and open and honest communication in a group. As such, it is employed proactively to establish group norms and relationships. It is also used in instances when it appears that that hidden agendas may be operating (e.g., people are sitting silently, eye contact is being avoided, people appear to be uptight).

The Process: A parking lot meeting is basically a process of advising a group that it is important to share what is on one's mind (particularly concerns that one might hesitate to share with an entire group) during the actual meeting. Steps for facilitating such emotional assessment and expression of concerns within the regular meeting—rather than later in the parking lot—are as follows:

1. Have participants form self-selected groups of three to five members and direct them to discuss whatever is on their minds regarding the topic(s) under discussion in the regular meeting in the next 5–10 minutes.

2. The parking lot meetings are to be conducted in a convenient space as selected by each group (a corner of the room, the hallway, or—if the location and weather cooperate—an actual parking lot).

3. At the end of the 5–10 minute period, reconvene the entire group and have each parking lot group share the gist of its conversation. Record issues and concerns raised on a transparency or flip chart.

4. After all the groups have shared the contents of their impromptu meetings, the whole group discusses the implications of expressed issues and concerns for productive adjustments in the meeting agenda and procedures.

The Payoff: The parking lot meeting activity exercises emotional intelligence through reflective interactions about what is of concern and what might be done about it. Emotional issues are surfaced and dealt with in a proactive fashion. The small-group configurations provide a safe environment for initial sharing about bothersome issues. The activity also structures physical movement, sharing of knowledge, and disposition to listen to and empathize with others.

The Practice: EIP.15. Conflict Resolution

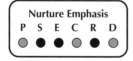

The Place: Conflict resolution is a practice that connects reflection about emotional states and advantageous options. It is a powerful approach that manages emotional arousal in a manner that exercises multiple dimensions of intelligence. It is a process that is applicable to any context that requires the evaluation of emotional states in the process of resolving conflicts.

The Process: While there are a variety of approaches to conflict and controversy resolution (e.g., as described in Chapter 7), elements common to most involve defining the issue, describing conflicting positions or perspectives, examining associated emotional states, establishing a rationale for a position or perspective, sharing and understanding opposing positions or perspectives, exploring options for resolution, and seeking agreement. Following is a representative description of those elements in a process adapted from Johnson and Johnson (1988):

	Steps in Conflict Resolution										
1	3	5	7	9	11	10	8	6	4	2
My objective/position is . . .	My emotional state is . . .	The rationale for my objective/position is . . .	My understanding of your objective/position and your emotional state is	Some options are	Our agreement/solution is . . .	Some options are	My understanding of your objective/position and your emotional state is	The rationale for my objective/position is . . .	My emotional state is . . .	My objective/position is . . .

1. Individuals or groups alternately clarify the objectives or positions that define the point of potential conflict. Such positions describe what is important to people in a given situation and/or what is of greatest interest to them. They are positions that can usually be summed up in a brief statement of "what my/our objective/position is."

2. Individuals or groups alternately describe their emotional state (i.e., how they "feel") related to their objective position.

3. Individuals or groups alternately describe the rational for their objective/ position.

4. Individuals or groups alternately state (as accurately as possible) their understanding of the objective/position, emotional state, and rationale of the other party (e.g., what the other party wants and feels and why).

5. Individuals or groups alternately offer points of agreement or brainstorm options that might resolve conflicting positions/objectives.

6. From the offered points and brainstormed options, the involved individuals and groups determine a position/solution they can agree to.

The Payoff: Conflict is a natural and necessary part of life. Without the dissonance and discomfort associated with conflicting ideas or needs, there is no reason to question, acquire knowledge, or adopt productive habits of mind. A conflict, then, arouses emotional attention to a problem or issue. A conflict-resolution process acts on such arousal to structure conscious reflection about possible solutions. Moreover, the process engages social interaction, assessment of emotional states, knowledge construction, and reflective review and projection. It is also a means to manage stress and cultivate collaborative, analytic, and creative dispositions of mind.

Reader Reflection

With reference to the preceding story, this section provides the opportunity for reflection about the related knowledge constructions that are occurring in your brain about the nature and nurture of emotional capacity. To that end, the template that follows will facilitate a reflective response to three questions:

1. What do you now know about the emotional nature of intelligence?

2. What does this knowledge mean to you (i.e., what are the most important insights, conclusions, or implications that emerge from what you know)?

3. What action(s) will you pursue given what you know and judge to be important?

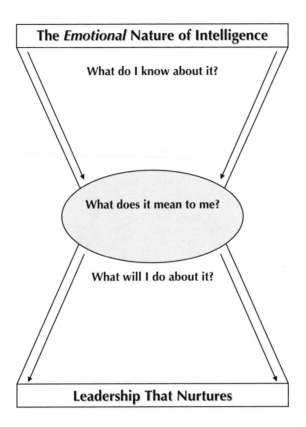

The *Emotional* Nature of Intelligence

What do I know about it?

What does it mean to me?

What will I do about it?

Leadership That Nurtures

6

Constructive Nature and Nurture

The Story of Constructive Capacity

Pat's brain is a pattern maker. It has a genius for putting things together. The story behind that genius is a strong survival interest in patterns that matter. To that end, Pat's brain is heavily invested in the knowledge construction business—a business that builds the neural networks behind perception, memory, language, music, art, and more. That business is not problem free, however, as Pat's brain must use multiple strategies and materials to avoid entrapment by patterns of limited or faulty design.

The Business

Knowledge is power. Pat's brain is in the pattern-construction business because the discernment of useful information patterns is the bottom line of survival. Indeed, the business of patterns has everything to do with what Pat's brain is and what it does.

Pat's brain is itself a product of pattern construction. It was assembled according to genetic patterns encoded in her DNA. That construction involved the precise organization of approximately 100 billion neurons, a trillion glial cells, and a multitude of other cellular and chemical compositions—producing the most complex construction on earth. In that process, some patterns were genetically installed in Pat's brain, such as neural networks dedicated to the recognition of geometric shapes, numbers, and the sounds of all the languages in the world. Most of the information patterns that Pat holds in her brain, however, have been put together throughout her life experience in response to environmental stimuli. Such constructions represent, among other things, all that she knows about people, history, literature, geography, economics, driving a car, and pizza.

Amazingly, Pat's brain began interpreting and integrating environmental patterns before it was done putting together the pattern of itself. Her neural predisposition to detect and connect information began to discern the patterns of beating hearts, breathing lungs, and moving blood while still in the womb. Shortly thereafter, she moved on to interpret rhythmic sounds emitted by hovering adults and visual patterns in faces. Thus Pat's brain began the business of connecting one pattern to another and another. It is a business that has grown to master language and reasoning and cultural norms. As Hart (1983) advised, it is a natural function that the brain does not have to be taught or motivated to do, any more than the heart needs to be instructed or coaxed to pump blood. It is a construction business that will continue throughout Pat's lifetime.

The pattern-making business that operates so naturally in Pat's brain is, of course, an inherited phenomenon—a business that is shared by all human brains. Notably, the success of this pattern-construction enterprise is heavily indebted to the mobility and social-emotional experiences of early operators.

Sylwester (2000) is among those who describe mobility as a defining property of human experience and a central reason for having a brain. To survive, organisms must recognize and remember information patterns, and the more mobile the organism the higher the premium that is placed on pattern recognition. It's a simple equation: Mobility expands the environmental experience of an organism, which in turn engenders more opportunity to detect and construct information patterns. The rule, it would appear, is that those who wander have greater opportunity and need to ponder.

At a basic level, the effect of mobility on pattern construction can be observed in early child development. Diamond and Hopson (1998) described the dramatic increase in neural activity and networking that occurs as children employ the four-point mobility system of crawling to expand their environmental reach and experience. The dramatic increase in sensory stimulation that results from such exploration provides a richness of data from which a child detects and connects patterns, thus feeding the construction of personal knowledge about objects, people, language, and how things work.

As very mobile organisms moving in social communities, Pat's ancestors had many reasons and opportunities to construct information patterns important to survival. The product of this rich construction experience over time was a socially adept and emotionally sophisticated big brain that was very good at the pattern organizing business.

In the twenty-first century, humans still move about in varied environments to feed the brain raw material important to the interpretation of patterns. The pattern-construction business today, moreover, is facilitated by computers, the Internet, and other media. Such technologies in themselves represent new information patterns for Pat's brain to master. Fortunately, the neural management team in her brain is up to the business at hand.

The Management

Given the extent and complexity of the task, the brain's pattern-making business is not attributable to a particular neural site, physiological structure, or dimension of intelligence. The acquisition and integration of important information patterns is the business of the entire brain. Accordingly, the physiological, social, emotional, reflective, and dispositional dimensions of intelligence collectively contribute to the construction of knowledge. In effect, the aforementioned qualities of intelligence form the management team that operates the pattern-making business in Pat's brain.

Physiological Management

Pattern construction operates at the cellular level on the biological platform of Pat's brain. Virtually every part of her brain is involved in this activity, but different sites have different interests. For example, Pat's amygdala screens information for patterns of emotional interest, her cerebellum is interested in patterns affecting procedural and automatic exercises of body or mind, and her hippocampus indexes patterns related to words, facts, and places. Information is also processed in Pat's primary and associated cortices (e.g., visual, auditory, motor), and her frontal lobes explore relationships between prior knowledge and new information.

Before any construction takes place anywhere in the brain, however, there must be construction material to work with. Such material comes to the brain in the form of internal and external sensory information. This is the fundamental key to Pat's pattern-construction ability—direct and multiple sensory inputs. The greater the intimacy and range of sensory information in the form of shape, sound, taste, smell, pressure, temperature, and movement, the more pieces of the puzzle her brain has to work with in the construction of meaning.

Given a rich supply of building material, then, the actual construction occurs when neurons that are stimulated by particular sensory input form alliances to acknowledge that information pattern. In effect, the neurons that are provoked to fire together, wire together (Hebb, 1949). Important to this phenomenon is that information patterns organized in well constructed neural alliances can be reengaged. Furthermore, the more frequently the pattern is activated, the more often the involved neurons access the cellular and chemical resources that support that neural alliance. In this fashion, a network becomes more strongly established—and memorable. It is, in effect, a "the more you use it, the better you build it and the less likely you are to lose it" construction process.

Social Management

Pat's brain both expects and depends on social interaction as a primary influence on the construction of valuable information patterns. Her brain particularly expects to construct information patterns through observing, mimicking, playing, listening, talking, debating, and many other social activities. The importance of such interaction cannot be overestimated. It is not only an important means for constructing understanding, but it is also the foil by which cognitive dissonance is generated and established patterns are challenged and refined. Vygotsky (1978), Slavin (1990), Johnson and Johnson (1999), and Marzano (2003) are among the many researchers who describe strong and lasting knowledge constructions as the products of highly interactive social experience.

Emotional Management

In effect, emotion decides what, where, and when pattern construction will take place. This is an essential element of Pat's pattern making because her brain cannot attend to and process everything. Accordingly, emotional networks screen and prioritize brain attention to information judged to be of some survival advantage. Emotion also influences the organization, storage, and retrieval of information patterns by the association of emotional context to the construction experience (e.g., pleasure, fear, excitement, anger, fun, sadness). More specifically, the construction of knowledge is enhanced by challenge and inhibited by threat (Caine & Caine, 1991). For example, stress states raise the level of the hormone cortisol in Pat's body, which has an adverse effect on information indexing in her hippocampus. In the other direction, the periodic release of noradrenalin in response to challenges Pat judges as achievable helps to focus and sustain her knowledge construction.

Reflective Management

The basic rule that guides Pat's neural pattern making is that things unknown become known when connected to things known. Accordingly, when her brain confronts information that is unfamiliar, its task is to establish a relationship to familiar patterns as a base for constructing new understanding. In this fashion knowledge is continually constructed and reconstructed in Pat's brain. The role of reflection in this business is to review the merits and the potential of information patterns. Such reflection occurs in Pat's frontal lobes as she mulls over information from sensory inputs of the moment in relationship to information from existing neural networks. It is a continuous process of explaining and exploring relationships between patterns—of analyzing, experimenting, projecting, formulating, and otherwise exploring how things work or might work. Thus, reflection is the means for refining and creating patterns through the conscious manipulation of the brain's rich information resources.

Dispositional Management

Dispositions are tendencies and inclinations that characterize one's thinking and behavior. The importance of disposition is revealed in the disparate manner in which individuals and groups exercise their capacity to acquire and apply knowledge. For example, Pat's brain cannot help but construct patterns. There is choice, nevertheless, in how she is disposed to conduct her pattern-making business. Pat might be disposed to maintain a healthy physiological brain state, manage emotion to advantage, seek out social stimulation, and frequently engage in reflective thinking strategies. Conversely, she might be disposed to abuse the physiology of her brain, let emotion range unbridled, withdraw from human contact, and think about things as little as possible. The point is, Pat has considerable leverage for shaping the dispositions that direct her behavior. She can either wait for pattern-making opportunities to come to her or she can proactively and aggressively seek out such opportunities.

The Problem

Knowledge is power because Pat's capacity to survive is born of her understanding of objects, people, events, processes, and abstract concepts. Such understanding arises from her brain's incessant detection and integration of useful information patterns. The good news for Pat is that her brain is very proficient at constructing serviceable information patterns. There is a problem, however, lying within that proficiency. The problem, according to Perkins (1995), is that Pat's brain is a "pattern machine" that becomes attuned through experience to familiar and useful patterns in the world— and adept at replaying such patterns efficiently and reflexively.

The double bind in the constructive works of Pat's brain, then, is that she is subject to bias toward patterns she is comfortable with. The danger of this circumstance is that Pat might inappropriately apply ingrained patterns to novel situations that require new understanding and an original response. Another dilemma is that her brain is capable of constructing a deficient information pattern based on limited or prejudiced experience. Both scenarios relate to Barker's (1992) warning about "paradigm paralysis" in human thinking: the trap of ill-founded certainty about established knowledge patterns (e.g., the earth is flat, women are not qualified to vote, smoking is not hazardous to one's health).

Fortunately, Pat's reflective and dispositional management of her knowledge construction—when exercised effectively—offers a means to avoid the double bind of her brain's pattern-making proclivity.

The Meaning of the Story

> *Perception is, in the end, a cognitive event. What we see is not simply a function of what we take from the world, but what we make of it.*
>
> —Eisner (2002, p. xii)

Pattern construction and recognition is the core business of Pat's brain. Without this foundational capacity, the other dimensions of her ability to learn and achieve are hopelessly compromised. Patterns represent the currency of Pat's brain. Patterns are what her brain values, accumulates, compounds, and exchanges. What is the meaning of this, then, for leadership? What leadership attention is due to this constructive quality of intelligence? A determination must be made, it is suggested, about what is most important to know and do regarding such capacity in self and others. For example, the genius, sensory, social, emotional, refined, and double bind nature of Pat's constructive brain might be particularly worthy of leadership attention.

Genius

The brain is a "lean, mean, pattern-making machine," a biological platform that has exceptional capacity for constructing meaning and memory from information patterns. The foundational genius of the human species is an extraordinary capacity for constructing and connecting useful information patterns. It is a capacity that underlies the cognitive processes by which all knowledge is acquired and how Pat's brain conducts the sophisticated work of language, abstraction, logic, metaphor, and imagination.

Sensory

The brain constructs meaning and memory from sensory input stimulated by environmental experience—and rich, direct experience influences the quality of construction. Beyond understanding and appreciating the pattern construction genius of Pat's brain, it is important to respect and accommodate how that genius conducts its business. That is, to do its best knowledge construction work, her brain requires a multisensory relationship with environmental information—to see, hear, touch, move, taste, and smell. Knowledge is very much a matter of construction, not instruction, and the more active, interactive, and multisensory the construction the better.

Social

Social interaction is a primary source of rich environmental experience that both stimulates and facilitates the construction of meaning and memory. There is no source more stimulating and helpful to Pat's knowledge-construction interests than interaction with other brains. Whether face-to-face or over distance and time, social experience is the great provocateur of knowledge construction and refinement.

Emotional

Emotion plays an important role in the construction of meaning and memory through the arousal of attention and the establishment of emotional context. Pat's brain only constructs understanding about information judged worthy of attention and effort. Emotion also enriches the construction information the brain has to work with, but positive tension enhances pattern construction, while excessive stress inhibits it.

Refined

What is constructed and remembered is reconstructed and refined by the brain through ongoing examination of relationships to new information. Knowledge is always a work in progress in Pat's brain. Every environmental experience she encounters is an opportunity for her brain to reference and adjust prior knowledge.

A Double Bind

Comfort with existing information engenders disregard for new information. Pat's brain values useful patterns as the means to survive and thrive. Useful mental models present a double bind, however, when openness to alternative patterns is ignored or resisted. The danger is that a familiar pattern will be maintained beyond its usefulness or accuracy. The necessary defense against such pattern complacency is a disposition to be open to new information and continually challenge and refine existing knowledge.

The Rest of the Story

Pat's story is about a genius for constructing meaning and memory—a genius influenced by sensory, social, and emotional experience, continually refined, and subject to a double bind. Genius (i.e., great natural ability), however, must be exercised to be potent. The rest of the story, then, is one of describing what might be done to nurture the nature of the constructive genius that resides in all individuals and organizations.

Mindful Strategy

Having constructed meaning about the pattern construction capacity of Pat's brain and every other healthy human brain on the planet, what might a leader do to nurture this powerful knowledge-construction business in self and others? Three strategies follow.

Strategy: Justify Construction

The brain is motivated to construct meaning and memory about information that is emotionally and rationally valued. With this in mind, a leader will structure assessments that establish the relevance and potential of new information.

Strategy: Facilitate Construction

The neural construction of meaning and memory is influenced by social interaction and other rich environmental experiences. Accordingly, a leader will facilitate the direct and multisensory engagement of diverse information sources.

Strategy: Extend Construction

Information patterns constructed and remembered are refined by connections to new information—if the brain does not become too comfortable with existing patterns. A leader will therefore seek to extend and refine established knowledge by promoting exposure to new information and challenges to established perceptions.

Mindful Practice

Pat's story comes to a close with descriptions of practices a leader might employ to nurture the constructive nature of her capacity for learning and achievement. The practices are aligned to strategies that aspire to (1) justify knowledge construction, (2) facilitate knowledge construction, and (3) extend knowledge construction. The practices presented are coded by an assessment of their primary (black), secondary (gray), and associated (white) influence on the physiological (P), social (S), emotional (E), constructive (C), reflective (R), or dispositional (D) nature of intelligence. As the pattern of this presentation format has been fairly well constructed in your brain by now, the practices offered are only examples of the 50 or more ways a leader might nurture the constructive genius of brain capacity.

Practices That Justify Construction

The brain is socially and emotionally aroused to construct meaning and memory. Accordingly, previously described practices that a leader might use to cultivate common purpose (e.g., before/after review or action planning as described in Chapter 4) or to excite the mind (e.g., an anticipatory set, mission set, or future set as described in Chapter 5) are also effective approaches to justifying knowledge construction. Following are additional practices that help the brain assess its knowledge interests.

The Practice: CIP.1. Preconstruction Assessment

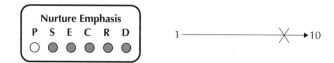

The Place: The brain has much to think about and must continuously assess what is worth knowing. Accordingly, a preconstruction assessment judges the potential and consequence of information before the learning begins—and this need not be complicated or time consuming for individuals or groups.

The Process: The process of assessing a learning opportunity can be as simple as pausing briefly to ponder the merits of new information. Such reflection might be structured by a concise sequence of questions as follows:

1. Does this information come from a credible source?

2. What is the research base for this information?

3. How is this information connected to what I/we already know?

4. How is this information related to my/our current mission/priorities?

5. How will I/we ever use this information in the future?

6. What is the best argument for pursuing this new knowledge?

7. What is the best argument for not pursuing this new knowledge?

The Payoff: The brain benefits from looking and assessing before jumping to new knowledge. Reflective analysis of the merits of a learning opportunity marshals emotional judgment and commitment. Deciding what is worth the allocation of its resources is an important brain decision. It is a decision that reflects the dispositions of being clear, analytic, and efficient.

The Practice: CIP.2. Construction Review

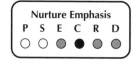

The Place: A construction review assesses what is known, what is to be learned, and learning progress. It is a means for individuals and groups to activate prior knowledge and set learning goals when engaging new information.

The Process: The basic steps of a construction-review process can be observed in an adaptation of the classic KWL (know-want to-learned) strategy (Ogle, 1986) that follows:

1. Determine the topic, issue, or body of knowledge to be addressed.

2. If conducting the activity in a large group, divide the group into smaller groups of three to six members.

3. Draw, distribute, or display the following graphic organizer (optional):

(1) What I/We Know	(2) What I/We Want to Know	(3) What I/We Will Do to Know It	Construction Zone	(4) What I/We Learned

4. Individuals reflect and record what they *know* about the topic, issue, or body of knowledge (i.e., Column 1).

5. If conducted in groups, small groups share what they know and report to the larger group (e.g., on transparency or flipchart copies of form) to compose a master list of the group's collective knowledge.

6. Individuals reflect and record what they *want* to know about the topic, issue, or body of knowledge (i.e., Column 2). If conducted in groups, repeat the small group to large group processing described under step 5 to compose a master list of information goals.

7. Individuals reflect and record what they *will do* to acquire the knowledge they desire or need (i.e., Column 3). This step focuses on procedures and resources that will be engaged. Again, if conducted in groups, small group to large group processing is employed to progressively discover and share resources and productive procedures.

8. Time is allocated (i.e., the construction zone) for pursuing resources and procedures prescribed under step 7 (e.g., 30 minutes to 30 days).

9. Individuals/groups reflect and record what they *learned* after pursuing prescribed resources and procedures for acquiring the targeted knowledge (i.e., Column 4). If conducted in groups, the small group to large group processing is repeated to share, clarify, and reinforce knowledge constructions.

10. After completing step 9 (depending on the dimensions of the knowledge engaged), individuals or groups adjust the prompt in step 6 to *what I/we want to know now* and then move through steps 6–9 again, repeating those steps as long as it is necessary and productive.

The Payoff: A construction review employs reflection about what is known and unknown to structure the connection of new knowledge to prior knowledge. When conducted in groups, the process taps the collective resources of a society of mind. It also promotes the proactive habits of collaboration, planning, organizing resources, and analytic thinking.

The Practice: CIP. 3. Mind Maps

Nurture Emphasis
P   S   E   C   R   D

The Place: A mind map explores the big picture of a topic (e.g., an introductory or summary review). It is a means to download prior knowledge about a topic or issue, thereby mapping out knowledge gaps and interests. It can be conducted individually or in groups.

The Process: This construction process maps the contents of the mind. Steps common to the multiple manifestations of the process are as follows:

1. Clarify the topic or issue to be explored (e.g., leadership, terrorism, flex scheduling, effective organizational cultures) and label and circle that focus at the center of a piece of paper, transparency, or a flipchart.

2. Brainstorm themes or categories around the focus (e.g., facts, events, causes, effects, pros, cons, types, timeframes, resources) and record them in spaces at some distance around the center circle.

3. Record information that comes to mind around each of the identified categories or themes.

4. Draw circles, squares, triangles, or other shapes around the themes, categories, and other recorded information with connecting lines between to show temporal, spatial, or conceptual relationships.

5. If working in groups, share and explain map content.

6. Ask and answer three questions:
   a. What do I/we know about this topic or issue?
   b. What don't we know and need to know?
   c. Where can we find what we need to know?

The Payoff: A construction map lays out the knowledge terrain in the brain. The practice incorporates a multisensory approach to plotting what is known and not known and what knowledge reconnaissance is in order. It is an emotionally comfortable process for mapping where one is and needs to be. It also initiates the reflective exploration of connections within and between existing knowledge and new information. The practice further encourages the dispositions of being organized, analytic, and open-minded.

Practices That Facilitate Construction

All the social intelligence practices that support meetings of minds and extend the mind's reach (e.g., dyads, jigsaws, corner conversations, book groups, and mentor relationships as described in Chapter 4) are powerful influences on the construction of knowledge. The practices that support the reflective and dispositional exercise of intelligence (as described in Chapters 7 and 8) also favorably influence the construction of knowledge. With reference to those 40 plus practices, then, some additional approaches to putting together the pieces of useful information patterns follow.

The Practice: CIP.4. Sensory Engagement

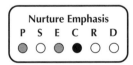

The Place: Sensory engagement with information is always important to the construction of meaning and memory. The brain is equipped with powerful knowledge-construction tools. What it needs to make effective use of those tools is quality construction material. The essential suppliers of such material are touch, taste, smell, sight, hearing, and movement.

The Process: Sensory engagement is a process of deciding how the brain will have direct (e.g., hands-on, eyes-on, ears-on) encounters with information. The idea is to judiciously involve multiple senses in the knowledge construction experience. A series of questions guides the process:

1. How can relevant information be experienced visually (e.g., print, film, video, Internet, artwork)?

2. How can relevant information be experienced by sound (e.g., lecture, conversation, story, music, film, video)?

3. How can relevant information be experienced by touch and movement (e.g., manipulatives, textures, drawings, dance, acting, constructions)?

4. How can relevant information be experienced by taste and smell (e.g., excursions, field trips, food, aroma)?

Following those initial questions, the process further contemplates the integration of sensory experiences. For example,

5. How can the engagement of relevant information be a "show and tell" (i.e., an integration of visual and auditory information).

6. How can the engagement of relevant information integrate physical movement and manipulation with visual and auditory experience?

The Payoff: In the business of constructing meaning and memory, the general rule is the more sensory the experience, the better. One must be aware of the danger of sensory overload and superfluous stimulation, but having a wealth of diverse information gives the brain more to work with when trying to figure out the patterns that matter. The built-in novelty of multisensory experience is also important to emotional attention and the robust engagement of the brain's physiological assets.

The Practice: CIP.5. Construction Pauses

The Place: A construction pause structures time for the brain to progressively and actively process information. It can be used individually and in groups in any setting where new information is being shared.

The Process: The basic process of a construction pause is to periodically stop (e.g., every 10–20 minutes) for a short period of time (e.g., 2–5 minutes) within a presentation or other engagement of information to actively process patterns of understanding that are forming in the brain. This is a process that can easily be conducted more than 50 ways. It is a process that periodically suspends a more passive learning mode (e.g., listening) to more actively engage the brain in the construction of knowledge. For example, individuals or small groups might be directed to pause for a few minutes within a presentation to (1) summarize, (2) clarify, (3) fill in gaps, (4) question, (5) answer questions, (6) draw graphic representations, (7) provide examples, (8) make comparisons, (9) identify resources, (10) calculate, or (11) project.

The Payoff: A construction pause naturally engages physical movement and emotional attention. Most important, however, it embrace the neural reality that learning is a matter of construction rather than instruction. That is, a brain has to construct its own understanding of the information it encounters, and it best conducts such construction by actively interacting with information (e.g., by talking, writing, drawing, calculating, comparing, and physically manipulating). Construction pauses also contribute to stress management by reducing extensive content to digestible pieces. Furthermore, they promote the dispositions of being accurate, clear, and focused.

The Practice: CIP.6. Construction Notes

The Place: Note taking of any sort is helpful to the brain when it is engaging new information. Construction notes provide a multisensory element to the organization of information into useful patterns that facilitate understanding and memory.

The Process: The process of note taking is, of course, conducted in many ways. Construction notes, however, assume a more structured and multisensory approach. One such example, as adapted from Marzano and Pickering (1997), is organized in the following graphic:

Topic:	Date:
Written Notes:	Graphic Representations:
Summary:	

The Payoff: Beyond an immediate effect on physical and emotional engagement, construction notes employ multiple senses and procedures to help the brain find and refine important information patterns. The process engages information visually and kinesthetically (and, it is assumed, auditorily). It also structures a fourfold processing of information (i.e., seeing and/or hearing it, writing it, drawing it, and summarizing it). Such processing further promotes the dispositions to be organized, analytic, and creative.

The Practice: CIP.7. Graphic Organizers

The Place: Similar to construction notes, graphic organizers provide multisensory assistance to the brain's organization of useful information patterns.

The Process: The process behind a graphic organizer is one of organizing a visual representation of essential information. Such a representation can be organized many ways, and Senge, Kleiner, Roberts, Ross, and Smith (1994); Marzano and Pickering (1997); and Parry and Gregory (1998) are sources for an array of examples. A few standard formats follow.

Concept Web: Useful for describing and organizing essential information about a topic or issue

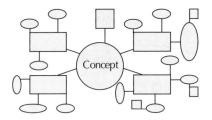

Venn Diagrams: Useful for making comparisons and/or identifying key components

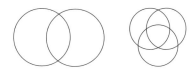

Sequence Map: Useful for organizing the order of events or the steps in a procedure

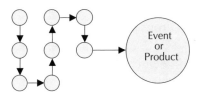

Fishbone diagrams: Useful for describing and organizing a pattern of sequential events and/or contributing influences

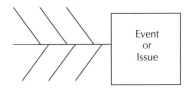

Pictograph: Useful for the simple, powerful reason that a picture *is* worth a thousand words when constructing meaning and memory

The Payoff: Graphic constructions of important knowledge components are physically and emotionally engaging. They also enlist multisensory experience with information, thereby giving the brain more material to work with and reflect about. The process also encourages the dispositions of being organized, analytic, and creative.

The Practice: CIP.8. Guiding Questions

```
Nurture Emphasis
P   S   E   C   R   D
○   ○   ◐   ●   ◐   ◐
```

?

The Place: Guiding questions clarify knowledge target(s) for individuals and groups. They are advanced organizers that prioritize knowledge and focus learning efforts in meetings, classrooms, or task groups.

The Process: The process behind guiding questions is one of formulating specific questions to be answered at the end of the day (i.e., session, meeting, week) regarding a topic, issue, or procedure. Such questions are generally organized around the classic inquiries of who, what, when, where, why, and how. To serve their focusing purpose, however, they must be specific to what is worth knowing about a particular information base. Generic examples of such questions an individual or a group might ask in advance of a learning effort would be

1. Who is an authority about _____ and what would he/she tell us?

2. What are the primary components of _____?

3. What are the steps in the process of _____?

4. What does _____ look like when done well?

5. When and where is the best time to _____?

6. What is the evidence that supports or questions _____?

7. What was the sequence of events that led to _____?

8. What has influenced/is influencing _____?

9. What are the cost factors associated with _____?

The Payoff: There is more to know than can be known, so the brain benefits from questions that establish what is most important to know. Clarity about a knowledge goal arouses the brain to emotional attention, while at the same time protecting it from the stress of confusion or feeling overwhelmed. Having a knowledge focus also promotes reflective analysis and synthesis and the dispositions to be focused, organized, and resourceful.

The Practice: CIP.9. Knowledge Expeditions

The Place: Knowledge expeditions identify and access resources that correspond to knowledge needs, emphasizing direct encounters with rich information.

The Process: The process of a knowledge expedition is to (1) identify a knowledge need (e.g., a guiding question), (2) identify rich sources of information related to the targeted knowledge (e.g., a person, site, event, body of literature, video, the Internet, or combinations thereof), (3) access sources to collect information (e.g., interview, observation, review of literature, Internet search), and then (4) organize and share findings.

The Payoff: The brain does its best knowledge construction work when emotionally committed and physically involved. That is, knowledge directly targeted and constructed by the brain is truly owned by the brain. Such construction also promotes social reflection, refinement of prior knowledge, and the disposition to be resourceful.

The Practice: CIP.10. Reciprocal Teaching

The Place: Teaching is a natural and powerful means for constructing understanding of any topic, issue, or process—thus the time-honored expression, "you never learn anything so as well as when you teach it to others."

The Process: Teaching is a process of assisting the learning of another or others. It is of assumed benefit to the knowledge acquisition of those on the receiving end. It is also a process, however, that benefits the teacher, as his or her knowledge is organized, reinforced, and refined by the act of teaching. Reciprocal teaching, then, aspires to capitalize on both ends of the teaching process. It does so by having individuals involved in learning about a new topic or process periodically "teach" each other (e.g., in dyads or triads) what they have learned or are learning (e.g., through summary explanations or demonstrations, description of examples or applications, posing or answering questions).

The Payoff: Facilitating the learning of another assumes physical engagement, social interaction, emotional commitment, and prior knowledge on the part of the facilitator. Most important to the construction of personal knowledge, the teacher must necessarily organize and integrate knowledge in his or her brain prior to facilitating such constructions in the brains of others. The act of teaching also necessitates reflection about options and strategies, as well as the dispositions to be organized, analytic, and creative.

The Practice: CIP.11. Reciprocal Views

The Place: A reciprocal view is a shorthand version of reciprocal teaching. It is a practice that cuts to the bottom line of what has been or is being constructed in the brain. It useful for clarifying and sharing knowledge at the beginning or ending of a meeting or learning event.

The Process: The general idea of a reciprocal view process is to share the views constructed in two different brains. This is done as a preview or review of a particular topic, issue, or process. The steps in the process are

1. Participants organize into pairs and identify each other as A or B.

2. A statement or question is presented to prompt prior knowledge at the beginning of a session or solicit summarization of knowledge at the end of a session (e.g., What do you already know about this? What do you expect to learn? What questions do you have about this? What did you learn? What is most important to remember about what was presented and discussed today? What are the basic steps in the process that was described and demonstrated? How will you apply what was presented and discussed? What questions do you have now?).

3. A presents an uninterrupted 2-minute oral response to the prompt while B listens with the intent of summarizing what A says.

4. B provides an oral 1-minute summary of what A said.

5. The process is repeated with A and B reversing roles.

The Payoff: The reciprocal review process structures reflective construction and refinement of knowledge through a social dialogue that is emotionally comfortable and focused. Participants reinforce and extend their understanding by bringing into view their perceptions and questions.

Talking for two uninterrupted minutes constructs personal meaning about the topic. Paraphrasing facilitates the understanding and incorporation of additional knowledge. It also promotes the disposition to listen carefully.

The Practice: CIP.12. Memorization

The Place: Memorization strategies facilitate the neural storage and retrieval of information. Memory is a natural product of knowledge construction. The retention and recall of particular information, however (e.g., names, steps in a process, key components), can be enhanced by specific strategies.

The Process: Memorization accents the natural memory process. It proactively constructs accessible information patterns in the brain by integrating linguistic, visual, physical, and emotional references. You remember a person (e.g., your mother, boss, or best friend), a thing (e.g., car, dog, or pasta dish), an event (e.g., wedding, tragedy, or big game), or a process (dancing, word processing, tax filing) because you have a combination of language (verbal and written), visual, physical, and emotional information that strongly references those patterns in your brain. Knowing this about the nature of memory, all memorization strategies employ linguistic, visual, physical, and emotional references (the more and more integrated, the better) to establish and access specific information in the brain. There are many such memorization strategies [e.g., as described by Marzano and Pickering (1997)], and some are more appropriate to some information targets than others. A few examples follow.

Remembering Names. A few brain-friendly tips for how leaders might better remember the names of people met for the first time are

1. *Pay attention.* Most often when you experience difficulty in recalling the name of someone you have just been introduced to, it is because you were not listening in the first place—perhaps distracted by introducing yourself or your visual attention to the other person. If and when this happens, immediately remedy the situation by admitting to

the information snafu (e.g., I'm sorry, my mind didn't completely register your name).

2. *Use the name.* Hearing a name once doesn't give the brain much to work with. You remember your mother's name because you have heard, said, and written it many times. Accordingly, immediately using the persons name (e.g., I'm pleased to meet you, Joanne) and subsequently using the person's name in conversation (e.g., Joanne, what are your thoughts about the leadership connection to the brain?) reinforces the initial information pattern.

3. *Mentally rehearse names.* Periodically repeat the name(s) of individuals who are new to you in your head as you look at them. This is particularly useful to remembering new names in a group.

4. *Make associations.* Visually associate the name and person with a familiar place and/or person (e.g., Nancy Stanford-Blair having tea at Stanford University with Tony Blair) or objects (e.g., Anthea Rosati-Bojar holding a rose in a jar).

Remembering What to Say. Leaders in classrooms, meetings, and other assemblies are often called upon to speak to an issue without benefit of teleprompters or notes. The loci memory strategy of locating objects or ideas in familiar locations is useful in such situations (e.g., as used by the ancient orators of Greece and Rome). This process is simply one of visualizing the sequential placement of objects, key points, or ideas at specific sites in a location one is familiar with (e.g., the furnishings in a bedroom, rooms in a house, buildings in a neighborhood, structures in a meeting room). In the case of making a statement or presentation, the brain visits the relevant sites to retrieve what has been stored there.

Remembering Things and Events. When it is desirable to more aggressively organize retrievable information in the brain, three additional strategies for doing so are

1. *Mnemonics.* A mnemonic is a device (e.g., an acronym, word, or phrase) that references information to be remembered. For example, HOMES is useful for referencing the five Great Lakes of Huron, Ontario, Michigan, Erie, and Superior. The usefulness of mnemonic devices is that they can be creatively constructed and applied to any content. Thus, the dispositional, reflective, social, physiological, emotional, and constructive dimensions of intelligence might be referenced in one's mind— with apologies to the good baby doctor—as DR SPEC.

2. *Story links.* A story is a fundamental means by which the brain organizes and communicates information. Thus the linking of substitute symbols into a story sequence is useful for remembering key information. For example, one might compose a story as follows: The *octopus* and the *piranha* hid in the *temple* by the *front* lawn of the *motor* court while trying to make *sense* of their dilemma. The substitute symbols in that story provide the brain with linguistic, visual, physical, and emotional hooks for progressing from the back to the side to the front to the top of the brain and identifying the six major regions of the cerebral cortex: The *occipital* lobes, *parietal* lobes, *temporal* lobes, *frontal* lobes, *motor* cortex, and *sensory* cortex

3. *Peg words and symbols.* The idea behind this strategy is to "hang" things you want to remember on the "pegs" of a framework previously committed to memory. As in the case of mnemonics and story links, such frameworks can be constructed and tailored to the needs and preferences of the individual brain. Peg words framed around a classic children's nursery rhyme provide an example of the process:

One	= *Bun*		Six	= *Sticks*
Two	= *Shoe*		Seven	= *Heaven*
Three	= *Tree*		Eight	= *Gate*
Four	= *Door*		Nine	= *Line*
Five	= *Hive*		Ten	= *Hen*

Pegs of words or symbols can accommodate large amounts of information. The process, nevertheless, is always one of envisioning an interaction between an item to be remembered and a peg word/symbol—and the more graphically visual, physical, and emotional the interaction the better. For example, to remember six defining characteristics of the constructive dimension of intelligence (i.e., genius, sensory, social, emotional, refined, and double bind), one might envision: (1) Albert Einstein arranging buns in the pattern of $e = mc^2$; (2) feet in shoes that are offensive to the senses by being unpleasantly tight, tattered, and pungent; (3) a social quilting or barn-raising event beneath a large oak tree; (4) a procession of graduates in caps and gowns alternately laughing and crying as they march out a door with diploma in hand; (5) a beekeeper refining honey through a honeycomb press in front of a busy bee hive; and (6) sticks attached to shoes with double-tied shoe strings.

The Payoff: The best way to remember something is to learn it well, because what is well learned is well remembered. For that reason, too much is often made of superficial memorization at the expense of quality learning that results in deep understanding. Nevertheless, it is valuable to have some strategies at one's disposal that employ direct and multisensory experiences to store and retrieve particularly important information. Such strategies are easily applied if and when warranted. They also promote the disposition to be analytical about what is worthy of further reflection and refinement.

The Practice: CIP.13. Modeling

The Place: Little is of more use to the brain in any effort to construct meaning than a good model. Seeing, hearing, or otherwise experiencing the finished product is like seeing the picture on the puzzle box: You know what it is supposed to look like after all the pieces are put together.

The Process: Modeling is a process that reveals the targeted information pattern to the brain before the brain attempts to construct it itself. It provides orientation and focus, particularly when learning a new procedure. While modeling is not complicated, it is important to appreciate the many ways it might be employed to advantage. For example, the construction of knowledge about a new procedure or program might benefit from modeling in the form of

1. A display of an exemplary product of a procedure or program

2. Written and graphic descriptions of sequential steps in a procedure

3. A demonstration of a procedure or program component

4. An expert performance of a procedure or program component

5. A scaled rubric describing the qualities of a procedure or program component when performed well, adequately, or poorly

6. Review of multiple procedure or program descriptions, examples, and demonstrations through literature, video, the Internet, or other media

7. Site visits to observe procedures and programs in reality contexts

The Payoff: Modeling provides the brain with an initial template from which to begin its construction work. It is a practice that promotes emotional focus and the social dispositions of observing, listening, questioning, and sharing.

The Practice: CIP.14. Practice

The Place: Practice makes perfect. If you want to master any skill or procedure, you know what you must do—practice, practice, practice. It matters not whether the target is a new program, protocol, technology, or technique. If you are going to ride the bike well, you have to ride the bike until you can.

The Process: It might appear redundant to identify practice as a practice, but this important element of constructing knowledge—particularly knowledge of procedures and skills—must not be overlooked. Essentially, it is a process of cultivating a desirable behavior or skill by exercising that very behavior or skill (e.g., as associated with listening, writing, coaching, technology, problem solving, decision making, planning, creative thinking). Decisions about a specific practice regimen will be context driven, but three general guidelines are

1. Individuals and groups benefit from being guided through practice steps and receiving feedback about their learning progress.

2. Short, intense, highly active practice sessions are more productive than long drawn-out practice sessions.

3. Massed (i.e., more frequent) practice should be scheduled at the beginning of learning a new skill or procedure. As mastery develops, practice periods can be distributed (i.e., less frequent and farther apart) to promote retention and refinement:

Massed Practice – ///// / / / / / / / / / – Distributed Practice

The Payoff: The neural networks that compose knowledge are tenuous and incomplete in the beginning stages of learning. Practice physically reinforces and refines initial neural constructions. Scheduled and structured practice also maintains emotional focus and the disposition to be persistent.

Practices That Extend Construction

Again, virtually all the social-intelligence aligned practices that support meetings of minds, cultivate common purpose, and extend the mind's reach (e.g., pair shares, jigsaws, corner conversations, book groups, action planning, and mentor relationships as described in Chapter 4) are powerful approaches to extending and refining knowledge. Similarly, practices that excite and evaluate states of mind (as described in Chapter 5), structure and challenge thinking (Chapter 7), and exercise and target productive dispositions of mind (Chapters 8) also offer processes that strongly influence the refinement of knowledge. With reference to the qualities of those practices, then, additional approaches that help the brain add pieces to the knowledge puzzle follow.

The Practice: CIP.15. Knowledge Updates

The Place: The brain naturally refines established patterns within its neural networks through encounters with new information (e.g., anytime you observe what is occurring around you, have a conversation, turn on the TV, listen to the radio, surf the Internet, or read a book or newspaper). This natural process is focused and enhanced, however, by proactive knowledge updates that target a particular knowledge base (e.g., information about leadership, learning, standards, assessment, planning, security, or technology).

The Process: Updating existing knowledge is simply a matter of accessing and connecting new information to prior knowledge. It is a process that becomes much more productive, nevertheless, when consciously employed to integrate current knowledge about specific fields, topics, issues, and procedures. A few examples of the many ways that such proactive updating of essential knowledge might be approached are

1. Regular reflection and conversation around the question: What currently extends or challenges what we know about _____?

2. Periodic participation in relevant seminars and workshops

3. Ongoing scans of diverse media (e.g., books, periodicals, video, Internet) to access and process important new information

4. Opportune interaction with authorities (e.g., authors, researchers, consultants) who offer expertise about current developments

The Payoff: The refinement of understanding is a never-ending endeavor. The structured updating of knowledge promotes social interaction and emotional focus. It also invites reflection while encouraging the dispositions to be inquisitive, resourceful, and open to new information.

The Practice: CIP.16. Comparison

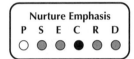

The Place: Comparison is a natural and powerful means by which the brain constantly refines its knowledge of the world. It is a useful practice, therefore, for consciously assessing the similarities and differences between items (e.g., people, issues, ideas, books, programs, procedures).

The Process: The process of comparison is one of describing and contrasting two or more items to discriminate common and differentiating qualities. It is a process that will vary according to particular formats and applications, but the basic steps (as applicable to either of the two graphic organizers on the following page) are as follows:

1. Identify the items to be compared.

2. Determine the criteria (i.e., attributes, qualities, characteristics) that will be compared (e.g., main events, primary components, key ideas, basic steps, customs, physical features, costs).

3. Provide descriptions of items to be compared according to criteria.

4. Describe similarities or commonalities between items.

5. Describe differences between items.

6. Summarize and discuss new insights and/or conclusions.

Venn Diagram Comparison (Two Items)   *Grid Comparison (Multiple Items)*

Item Description:	Item Description:

Differences: Similarities: Differences:

Item:	Item:	Item:
Describe:	Describe:	Describe:

Commonalities

| Unique Features | Unique Features | Unique Features |

The Payoff: Comparison is how the brain naturally differentiates and refines information patterns. It is the process by which children discover the discriminating characteristics between a dog and a cat. The same process is at work when the brain is discerning similarities and differences in policies, procedures, and programs. It is a reflective process by which the brain is disposed to extend and refine basic understanding, as well as the dispositions to be analytic and seek clarity.

The Practice: CIP.17. Progressive Jigsaw

Nurture Emphasis
P   S   E   C   R   D

The Place: A progressive jigsaw draws from the same research base (e.g., Aronson, Stephan, Sikes, & Snapp, 1978; Slavin, 1990; Johnson & Johnson, 1999) and serves the same general purpose as a basic jigsaw (i.e., Practice SIP.5). That is, it structures the collaborative learning of divisible information (e.g., the contents of books, chapters, reports, or conceptual models). A progressive jigsaw is preferable, however, when time and circumstance allow for the more extended and refined construction of knowledge in groups.

The Process: A progressive jigsaw can be structured and conducted in many ways. The universal quality of the process, however, is that it provides progressive and extended opportunities to refine knowledge as it is being constructed. An example of the process is

Organization of Triads

1. A larger group is divided into numbered triads (i.e., 1–3) and presented with or directed to relevant information sources.

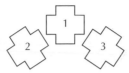

2. Each numbered member in each triad is assigned a specific portion of targeted content (i.e., all the 1s, 2s, and 3s have the same content).

Task Assignment

Each member of each triad is to:

1. Construct personal understanding of assigned content

2. Explain/teach the assigned content to others

Preparation

1. Each triad member individually reviews assigned material to identify key content and organize ideas about how to explain/teach it to others.

2. Individuals partner with someone from another triad who has the same number/content assignment to (1) share their understanding of content and (2) plan how to explain/teach it to others.

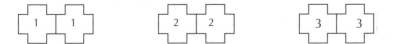

Practice

Individuals form a second partnership with someone from another triad who also has the same number/content assignment to practice the explanation/teaching approach prepared with their first partners.

Presentations in Triad

1. Individuals reform their original triads and progressively explain/ teach their understanding of assigned content within set time limits.
2. Triad members conduct follow-up discussions to raise questions and further clarify understanding of content.

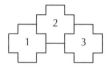

Whole-Group Processing

Triads share essential information, key insights, and questions with the whole group.

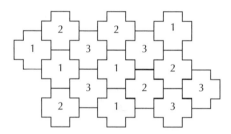

The Payoff: An extended jigsaw process further engages the brain's bias for learning through direct social interaction. As described above, it is a process that structures direct interaction with targeted content multiple (i.e., five to six) times. Thus, it maintains emotional attention while progressively constructing and refining understanding. It also promotes the dispositions to listen, question, be creative, cooperate, and plan well.

The Practice: CIP.18. Role-Plays

The Place: Role-plays are powerful vehicles for internalizing and communicating refined understanding of specific information.

The Process: A role-play involves assuming the role of a specific or representative individual for the purpose of acquiring associated knowledge. It is useful when the participation of the real deal is not possible (e.g., Mohandas Gandhi, W. Edwards Deming, Howard Gardner, Peter Senge, Margaret Wheatley, or Alan Greenspan). Participants can also assume the role of a representative "authority" on a topic (e.g., a fictional expert on total quality management, organizational planning, school improvement, facility security, performance coaching, academic standards, systems thinking, performance assessment, infectious disease protocols, or a particular technology). Obviously, then, this is a process that has unlimited possibilities. The basic steps, nevertheless, are

1. Establish the purpose of the role-play (i.e., the targeted knowledge).

2. Assign the role(s) and preparation/presentation schedule.

3. Access relevant information and otherwise prepare the role-play.

4. Play the role in the appropriate context (e.g., small group, meeting, classroom) to share acquired expertise about the targeted knowledge.

5. Debrief the role-play for insights gained and questions that remain.

The Payoff: A role-play takes reciprocal teaching (i.e., CIP.10) to the next level by structuring a more intimate relationship with targeted knowledge. Assuming the role of a specific or generic authority is a very social experience that fosters emotional engagement and focus. Most important, the responsibilities of a role-play encourage the extended construction of knowledge in anticipation of questions and challenges. The practice also encourages the dispositions of planning, persistence, and creativity.

The Practice: CIP.19. Extended Conversations

The Place: Extended conversations structure the progressive processing of targeted knowledge through self-scheduled meetings with multiple partners. It is useful to the initial construction of new knowledge, as well as the refinement of knowledge over compacted or extended periods of time. It is a practice that can be conducted with any group size of three or more.

The Process: An extended conversation is structured by the following steps:

1. A knowledge target is determined (e.g., a topic or issue).

2. Participants are instructed to schedule appointments with a specified number (e.g., three to six) of members of the group at specific times (e.g., within a meeting, every half hour; within a day, 9:00 A.M., noon, and 3:00 P.M.; within a week, Monday, Wednesday, and Friday at 4:00; within a month, Wednesdays at lunch; or within a year, quarterly).

3. Participants meet at their scheduled appointments to share their current understanding and experience with the targeted knowledge.

The Payoff: Extended conversations structure an emotionally comfortable refinement of knowledge through dialogue. Such activity broadly engages the brain's dependency on social interaction with other brains to do its best work. Conversation also promotes the disposition to listen, seek clarity, and integrate the insights of others.

The Practice: CIP.20. Extended Coaching

The Place: Extended coaching provokes reflection and provides feedback between participants (e.g., two to three) about progress made in mastering new information and procedures. It is a practice that facilitates the extension and refinement of knowledge while learning is in progress.

The Process: The process of extended coaching is a more formal and structured version of an extended conversation (i.e., CIP.19). The steps in the process—as conducted within the ideal dynamics of a coaching triad—are as follows:

1. Participants organize into triads and identify each member as A, B, or C (encourage the formation of triads that reach outside of base groups or departments to increase diversity of experience and insight).

2. Each triad arranges a time and space that accommodates face-to-face interaction within a comfortable listening proximity (e.g., three chairs facing inward or arranged around the end of a table).

3. A presents information about his or her current understanding or experience with the targeted knowledge or skill while B and C take notes and prepare to give feedback.

4. B and C provide feedback to A in the form of
   a. Summarization of what they heard A say
   b. Questions they may have
   c. Suggestions they may have

5. A provides feedback to B and C about their coaching contributions (i.e., how well did they provide constructive feedback? What did they say or do that was most helpful?).

6. Steps 1–5 of the process are repeated with B and then C sharing information about their learning progress and experience.

The Payoff: The coaching process structures meaningful refinement of knowledge around professional dialogue, thereby engaging the brain's dependency on provocative social interaction with other brains to do its best work. The brain is physiologically stimulated by the novelty and movement within the activity, as well as emotionally aroused by the extended construction of knowledge. The activity also encourages the dispositions to listen carefully and to be positive, clear, and specific.

Reader Reflection

With reference to the preceding story, this section provides an opportunity for reflection about the related knowledge constructions that are occurring in your brain about the nature and nurture of constructive capacity. To that end, the template that follows will facilitate a reflective response to three questions:

1. What do you now know about the constructive nature of intelligence?

2. What does this knowledge mean to you (i.e., what are the most important insights, conclusions, or implications that emerge from what you know)?

3. What action(s) will you pursue given what you know and judge to be important?

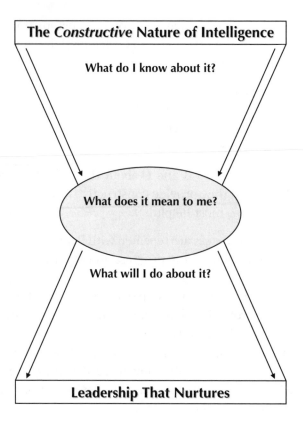

7

Reflective
Nature and Nurture

The Story of Reflective Capacity

Manuel's brain is a manipulator, distinguished by its capacity for analyzing, projecting, and otherwise massaging information. The story of Manuel's reflective brain reveals the neural stage upon which the drama of human reasoning occurs. It is also an account about how the collective resources of the brain are directed in the exercise of thinking.

The Stage

> *Imagination, that form of thinking that engenders images of the possible, also has a critically important cognitive function to perform aside from the creation of possible worlds. Imagination also enables us to try things out—again in the mind's eye—without the consequences we might encounter if we had to act on them empirically. It provides a safety net for experimentation and rehearsal.*
>
> —Eisner (2002, p. 5)

Manuel is heir to a brain that has dramatically extended its reach into the theater of the world. It is a brain that has literally expanded its physiological platform outward through the prolonged provocation of rich environmental experience. The product of this expansion is most profoundly represented in the frontal lobes of the cortex, the area of Manuel's neural landscape that he depends on to maximize brain capacity to resolve, create, and project. The significance of this neural area in the human story is difficult to exaggerate. Goldberg (2001, p. 24) labeled it "the organ of civilization."

The reflective nature of Manuel's brain is thought to have emerged most directly from the social evolution of brain capacity for information patterning, emotional awareness, and language. Calvin (1996) observed that the neural mechanism that enables the stringing together of meaningless phonemes to form meaningful words is the same mechanism that underlies the stringing together of words into sentences, concepts, and narrative stories. Ultimately, this stringing together of patterns is exhibited in Manuel's unique human capacity for stringing together mental narratives about events, issues, possible actions, and probable effects—that is, the capacity to analyze, plan, and predict. The development of neural networking in the prefrontal cortex, then, enabled conscious reflection about events and options. In effect, the brain developed the capacity to conduct a conscious conversation within itself—thus the stringing together of information patterns into words and sentences was paralleled by the stringing together of information patterns into abstractions and hypotheses. This reflective conversation is observed at the neural level in the outer layers of the prefrontal lobe, but it is a process that is intimately connected to Manuel's entire neural system.

The Drama

Capacity for conscious reflection is *the* distinguishing quality of Manuel's brain. His brain has a phenomenal capacity for constructing understanding of things the way they are, but it also has the capacity to reconstruct how and why they were as well as project how and why they might be. In the very big survival picture, this is the intelligence capacity that has made the defining difference for humankind. It is the difference associated with analytic and creative thinking—the thinking involved in everyday decision making, problem solving, questioning, experimentation, invention, forecasting, comparison, abstraction, and inductive and deductive thinking. It is the capacity to see and debate answers to questions of why and how and what if within the confines of one's own mind—to imagine.

Manuel's reflective capacity, then, is about enhancing the potential of information. Such reflection might be envisioned as a laser light show in his brain involving electrochemical messages flashing between trillions of synapses in incredibly complex arrangements of incoming, recalled, and reconstructed information patterns. This is the physical reality of "brainstorming." Evidence of this neural activity is visibly connected to the drama of exploration, investigation, coaching, directing, and planning. It is observable in the creativity and problem solving of artists, politicians, and entrepreneurs. The same process of mentally massaging existing information is at work in pursuing personal relationships, planning a vacation, or pondering a career move.

The Director

Manuel's frontal lobes evolved to coordinate the components of an increasingly complex brain. To that end, they are globally connected to the rest of his neural architecture to perform complex executive functions. The prefrontal cortex plays a central role in this process by forming goals, devising plans for attaining goals, coordinating the cognitive skills required to implement the plans, and then evaluating the success or failure of plan implementation (Goldberg, 2001).

In performing its executive role, then, Manuel's reflective brain directs the entire cast of his intelligence capacities in unified performances. Conscious reflection about a problem, decision, or other challenging task lights up neural networks throughout the physiological platform of Manuel's brain. In effect, his brain performs as a house of mirrors as it plays the light of new and established information among trillions of neural networks to explore and form options. Reflection seeks out the knowledge of other brains, through either direct or extended means. Social interaction is the great provocateur of reflection, the foil that challenges and refines existing patterns in the quest for the better pattern. Reflection fans the passions of the mind, thus generating the emotional focus and motivation required of sustained mental efforts. Similarly, reflection about a meaningful problem or other task motivates Manuel's brain to construct knowledge. He cannot reflect about alternatives and options without relevant information. Accordingly, information must either be retrieved from existing neural networks, or new patterns of understanding must be constructed if Manuel's brain is to compose its virtuoso performances of thought and deed. Finally, the exercise of reflective intelligence requires a disposition to analyze, create, and resolve. The establishment and refinement of such disposition, moreover, is the product of reflective-thinking experience—that is, practice, practice, practice.

The Meaning of the Story

The frontal lobes are to the brain what a conductor is to an orchestra, a general is to an army, the chief executive officer is to a corporation. They coordinate and lead other neural structures in concerted action.

—Goldberg (2001, p. 2)

Pattern construction and recognition is the core business of the brain, but reflective reasoning is the executive function that applies that business to exceptional advantage. Indeed, the reflective capacity of Manuel's brain is what defines the biological niche of humankind. It is the capacity by which individuals and groups can aspire to unravel any mystery, resolve any problem, and meet any challenge. It is *the* capacity that is inevitably of the greatest interest to leaders when the going gets tough and there are no set answers. What, then, is most worth knowing about this most exotic dimension of intelligence? The suggestion here is that leaders everywhere— whether in the schoolhouse, medical center, manufacturing plant, financial institution, or any other human enterprise—should understand and attend to how the brain is manipulative, executive, governing, unifying, and promising.

Manipulative

Reflection is the distinguishing brain capacity for consciously manipulating information and rehearsing options prior to action—to move beyond the construction of what is to the contemplation of what has been and might be. Manuel's brain is always working information to review actions and project events. This is "the essence of the essence" of intelligence and the most potent asset to be nurtured in any human system.

Executive

Reflection serves an executive function that purposefully accesses, coordinates, and directs the vast resources of the brain in the exercise of complex reasoning. Manuel's frontal lobes not only enable reflection, they also enable reflection about what is worth reflecting about and how the rest of the brain will be involved. This is the capacity by which neural assets are allocated and managed to a greater or lesser advantage.

Governing

Reflection constrains, redirects, or otherwise remedies actions initiated in other brain areas—particularly actions initiated in the emotional centers of the brain. Within the executive function of Manuel's reflective brain is a particularly valuable capacity for governing primal instincts. This is evident when rational reasoning is employed to harness the power of emotion to a productive advantage.

Unifying

Reflective attention to a meaningful problem or decision requires physiological support, social interaction, emotional tension, knowledge construction, and productive thinking dispositions. Reflective reasoning comprehensively engages the integrated neural networks of Manuel's brain. When confronted with a real world challenge, his brain is physically engaged, emotionally focused, and socially disposed toward the construction and refinement of information patterns that will resolve the issue.

Promising

The essence of reflection is expressed in scientific inquiry, philosophy, and art—it is the capacity that empowers human versatility and future prospects. Reflective analysis, experimentation, and imagination are the keys to human survival and success.

The Rest of the Story

Manuel's story describes the crowning glory of human intelligence, the reflective capacity to consciously manipulate information backward and forward and inside-out. It is a capacity that directs the complex thinking required in solving problems, improving programs, and creating new products and procedures. The rest of the story, then, explores strategies and practices that might be employed to nurture the nature of analytic and creative thinking in individuals and organizations. That is, how a leader might best "go for the gray" and connect to the reflective powers of the prefrontal cortex.

Mindful Strategy

In reflecting about the reflective capacity of Manuel's brain and all other healthy brains that you encounter in your social and professional life, what might you do to nurture that capacity in self and others? Two strategies follow.

Strategy: Structure Thinking

The brain will more efficiently engage in its natural capacity for manipulating information when facilitated by templates that structure particular kinds of thinking, such as templates that structure the steps in problem solving, decision making, or planning.

Strategy: Challenge Thinking

The best thinking takes place at the edge. The analytic and creative capacities of the brain are brought into play by serious questions in need of answers. That is, the brain will not bring forth its greatest assets unless pressed by the environment to do so.

Mindful Practice

The story of Manuel's reflective brain concludes with a description of 30 practices aligned to strategies that: (1) structure thinking and (2) challenge thinking. The practices are coded by an assessment of their primary (black), secondary (gray), and associated (white) influence on the physiological (P), social (S), emotional (E), constructive (C), reflective (R), or dispositional (D) nature of intelligence. The practices are, again, only examples intended to prod a leader's further reflection about the 50 or more things that might be done to nurture the reflective dimension of brain capacity.

Practices That Structure Thinking

The brain is socially and emotionally provoked to apply the executive functions of its frontal lobes to the manipulation and further construction of knowledge. Many of the previously described practices in Chapters 3–6 (i.e., practices a leader might employ to introduce novel experience, facilitate meetings of mind, cultivate common purpose, excite the mind, or extend the mind's reach and construction of knowledge) provide provocation and structure for reflective thinking. The following practices are examples of structures that are more directly dedicated to the proactive exercise of the reflective capacity of the brain.

The Practice: RIP.1. Problem Solving

The Place: A problem is any question or matter of uncertainty or difficulty related to a goal. Accordingly, there could hardly be any practice that would be of more universal interest and use to leaders than that of problem solving.

The Process: Problem solving is something the brain does all the time—whether resolving the challenges of preparing the evening meal or the mapping of the human genome. The natural process in such reflection involves

1. Identification of a problem

2. Contemplation of possible solutions

3. Deciding which solution is best and applying it to the problem

4. Accessing the effect of the attempted solution

When conducted more formally and done well by individuals or groups, the process involves the following steps:

1. Describe the goal (i.e., the desired result). This might seem simple enough, but such clarification is critical to the efficiencies and effectiveness of subsequent steps.

2. Describe the problem. That is, identify the conditions and circumstances that are creating uncertainty or difficulty or otherwise standing in the way of the described goal—the constraints and obstacles that define the problem.

3. Brainstorm possible solutions to the problem—ways to resolve or overcome the defining constraints and obstacles.

4. Determine and implement the most promising solution(s).

5. Assess the success of the attempted solution(s) and consider what further adjusted or alternative attempts are warranted.

The Payoff: A structured problem-solving process establishes emotional orientation to a compelling goal and a meaningful application of knowledge. It engages social interaction—direct, extended, or both—in the construction of knowledge and analytic and creative reflections. The process is particularly effective in provoking reflection about what is known and unknown about a problem and specific resources and procedures for resolving knowledge needs. Problem solving also exerts a strong influence on the productive thinking dispositions of listening, accessing resources, planning, and being open-minded.

The Practice: RIP.2. Decision Making

The Place: Decision making is a matter of making a determination or judgment, reaching a conclusion, or otherwise resolving a question or issue. Accordingly, it is intimately associated with problem solving—and another practice that is of universal interest and use to leaders.

The Process: Like problem solving, decision making is a pervasive brain activity. It is engaged when determining which toothpaste to purchase or which candidate to vote for. In its simplest form, it is a reflective process of

1. Identifying options

2. Assessing the relative merits of the available options

3. Selecting the most appealing option

When conducted in a formal manner, the process is more consciously attentive to criteria in assessing options. A graphic example as adapted from Marzano, Norford, Paynter, Pickering, and Gaddy (2001) follows:

1. Identify the decision to be made (e.g., a decision regarding staff development, software, consultant services, budget priorities).

2. Identify the alternatives to be considered.

3. Identify the criteria that will influence the assessment of alternatives.

4. Assign a value scale to the identified criteria (e.g., 1–3 = low to high).

5. Rate the extent to which each alternative meets each criterion by a value scale (e.g., 1–3 = low to high).

6. Multiply the criterion values and ratings for each alternative.

7. Total scores for each alternative and determine whether there is a clear decision or if further review of criteria and/or alternatives is required.

Decision to be made:			
Criteria	Alternatives		
	A. ———	B. ———	C. ———
1. ___ Value ☐	x Rating ☐ = ☐	x Rating ☐ = ☐	x Rating ☐ = ☐
2. ___ Value ☐	x Rating ☐ = ☐	x Rating ☐ = ☐	x Rating ☐ = ☐
3. ___ Value ☐	x Rating ☐ = ☐	x Rating ☐ = ☐	x Rating ☐ = ☐
Summary	Total ☐	Total ☐	Total ☐
Decision:			

The Payoff: The natural decision-making processes of the brain are emotionally focused and procedurally guided by a structured format. Conscious reflection about alternatives and criteria encourages social reflection and debate in the referencing and construction of knowledge. Individuals and groups will be more informed and involved in the analysis leading to a decision. Subsequently, they will realize ownership for decisions made and implemented. They will also reinforce the dispositions to listen, question, access resources, be objective, and discern relationships.

The Practice: RIP.3. Brainstorming

The Place: Brainstorming generates a rich pool of alternative ideas and options. It is commonly used in problem solving and decision making.

The Process: Brainstorming can be organized many ways and is often embedded within other reflective-thinking exercises. Informally, it can be as simple as composing a list of plausible explanations, examples, or actions. Whatever the format, however, the basic components of the process are as follows:

1. Participants generate and record as many ideas as they can in response to a stated problem or need (e.g., how to resolve a conflict, improve a program, or achieve a goal).

2. Ideas are offered spontaneously or in ordered fashion by participants, but the generation of ideas continues for the prescribed time limit (e.g., 5–15 minutes) or until no more ideas are forthcoming from the group.

3. Participants withhold judgment and conversation until all ideas are out. The point is to be open and creative and leave no avenue unexplored.

4. After the "storming," ideas are evaluated, combined, and refined.

The Payoff: It is better to tame wild ideas than to be devoid of any. The reflective brain is emotionally focused and socially provoked by brainstorming to access prior knowledge and project possibilities. The activity also promotes the dispositions of being open-minded, analytic, creative, and proactive.

The Practice: RIP.4. Progressive Brainstorm

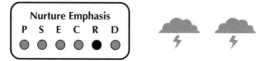

The Place: A progressive brainstorm is brainstorming that incorporates an added dimension of social provocation to pool the ideas of a large group regarding multiple questions or issues.

The Process: Two of the most common approaches to progressive brainstorms are

1. Move the ideas.
   a. Subgroups are formed and assigned separate questions or issues.
   b. Each group is provided with a large sheet of paper and markers.
   c. Subgroups generate and record as many ideas as they can in response to their problem or issue within a set amount of time.
   d. The sheets with stated problems or issues and recorded lists of ideas are rotated to other groups (e.g., clockwise).
   e. Subgroups read the question or issue and the ideas of the previous group on the sheet they receive and then add their ideas to the list.
   f. The process is repeated until each question/issue sheet has been processed and contributed to by multiple subgroups (e.g., 3–7).
   g. The lists are debriefed for themes and key ideas by the large group.

2. Move the brains.
   This approach is the same as "move the ideas," except that the sheets of paper remain in place (e.g., on tables or taped to walls) and subgroups rotate to the different sites to progressively contribute their ideas.

The Payoff: A progressive brainstorm adds another layer of social interaction to the brainstorming process. Individual brains are more immediately provoked by the ideas within and between groups in the process of generating alternative ideas. Participants are emotionally focused and socially engaged in the reflective compounding of information and possibilities. And, like brainstorming, the activity promotes the dispositions of being open-minded, analytic, creative, and proactive.

The Practice: RIP.5. Affinity Grouping

The Place: Affinity grouping facilitates reflection about similarities and difference in issues discussed and ideas generated. It is a useful practice for analyzing, organizing, and displaying the products of large group brainstorming.

The Process: Affinity grouping is a process of discerning prominent patterns within a wealth of brainstormed ideas. It organizes an abundance of insight by "affinities" (i.e., commonalities). It is a process that reduces the collective wisdom of a large group to a manageable number of important ideas that then guide subsequent decisions and actions. The general steps are as follows:

1. The question or issue to be addressed by the group (e.g., a prioritization of goals, work climate assessment, new technology, schedule revision, program implementation, mentoring options) is identified.

2. Brainstormed ideas and suggestions regarding the question or issue (e.g., 3–4 per person or 6–12 per subgroup as produced in a RIP.4 brainstorming activity as previously described) are individually recorded on large pieces of post-it paper or sheets of paper that can be taped, tacked, or otherwise arranged on a flat surface.

3. All the recorded ideas are collected and displayed on a flat surface.

4. The displayed ideas are rearranged by similarities (i.e., affinities) to create a graphic display of categories and frequency of like responses.

5. The group discusses the prominent categories and their implications for decisions and actions.

The Payoff: Affinity grouping engages a high degree of social interaction and emotional judgment in the pooling of knowledge and the reflective analysis of options and relationships. It also promotes the dispositions of being open-minded, analytic, creative, and collaborative.

The Practice: RIP.6. Nominal Group Process

The Place: The nominal group process further guides divergent ideas toward convergent perceptions in problem solving and decision making. It is a means to make group decisions about priorities following the brainstorming of ideas and the affinity grouping of prominent categories or themes. Accordingly, it is particularly useful in action planning groups.

The Process: Nominal group processing incorporates brainstorming and the discernment of prominent alternatives with the prioritization of subsequent decisions or actions. The essential steps in the process are

1. Clarify the goal of the process (e.g., to decide a need or action).

2. If used in a large group, form subgroups by random selection (to assure diversity of experience and ideas).

3. Select a group facilitator and secure paper, markers, and tape.

4. Brainstorm and record ideas related to the stated goal (e.g., to determine a need or action) within a given time limit.

5. Refine the recorded list by consolidating similar ideas. If subgroups are involved, post and share their refined lists of ideas with other groups.

6. If there are subgroups, ask clarifying questions about each group's list and consolidate the lists by similarities to generate a master list of ideas.

7. Each participant is given an allocation of points (e.g., 5–10) to be assigned to their prioritization of proposed ideas on the master list.

8. After all participant points have been assigned, the group prioritization of needs or actions emerges (this is made more graphic if point assignments are distinct hash marks or pasted dots on the master list).

The Payoff: A nominal group process structures productive social interaction and emotional focus in the sharing of knowledge and a collective analysis of greatest needs and best options. The process also promotes a number of valuable dispositions associated with effective collaboration, including listening and questioning, and being open-minded and creative.

The Practice: RIP.7. Consensus

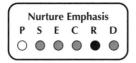

The Place: Consensus means there is general agreement about a particular position or decision that everyone can live with. It is a group agreement accepted by each member. As such, consensus building is another reflective-thinking practice that is helpful to problem solving and decision making—and, in the bigger picture, organizational planning and development. It is a practice, moreover, that is more deliberative in moving a group toward agreement about what is important and/or a strategic course of action.

The Process: The process of consensus is one of communicating ideas until there is general agreement about a topic, issue, or procedure. In its simplest form, this can be a matter of two people conversing until they agree about their understanding of something and what should be done about it. In a more formal fashion, the steps in the process might be structured as follows:

1. Clarify the definition of consensus as general agreement about a particular position or decision that everyone can live with.

2. Clarify the consensus goal (e.g., agreement about mission, standards, goals, strategies, or a specific course of action).

3. Establish rules of behavior for reaching consensus:
   a. Everyone has the right to state opinions and ask questions
   b. Everyone will be listened to with respect and courtesy

4. Individually reflect about ideas related to the consensus goal.

5. Engage in group dialogue (in subgroups of 3–5 if working with a large group) and brainstorm ideas related to the consensus goal.

6. Periodically check with members of the group to determine whether an idea or combination of ideas that everyone might agree to has surfaced in the dialogue, using some variation of the following procedure:
   a. If in agreement, signal thumbs-up
   b. If in disagreement, signal thumbs-down
   c. If less than satisfied but can live with it, signal thumb-to-the-side

7. If everyone agrees or can live with it, there is consensus. If not, continue the dialogue until progress warrants another consensus check.

The Payoff: Consensus decisions are more easily implemented because they evolve from a collective social-emotional commitment and wisdom. Consensus building constructs and refines knowledge in the process of reviewing and projecting alternative ideas. The process also promotes the reflective dispositions of being open-minded, analytic, creative, and proactive.

The Practice: RIP.8. Fish Bowl

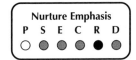

The Place: A fish bowl structures collective group reflection about a topic or issue. It is a highly interactive practice that is useful for generating ideas, sharing perceptions, or debating positions. It is a dynamic "real-time" approach to public thinking and learning that is adaptable to any group context.

The Process: The fish bowl process positions a portion of a group in the center of a room or area surrounded by the remaining members of the group.

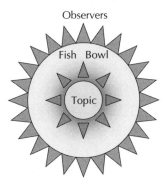

Members in the center (i.e., the fish bowl) are assigned a topic to discuss. Members positioned around the center group observe, listen, and take notes but do not participate. After a given discussion time has elapsed, the observers are invited to extend or question what was shared in the center group. Another approach is to invite members of the group to move to or from the fishbowl per their interest in being an active discussant or an observer at any time in the discussion. Regardless of the specific procedures employed, the entire group debriefs the discussion at the end.

The Payoff: A fish bowl facilitates both public and private reflection about complex issues. It accommodates a range of emotional states and social interaction. It is also very inviting of diverse experience and expertise, as well as the dispositions of being a good listener, open-minded, analytic, and creative.

The Practice: RIP.9. Force Field Analysis

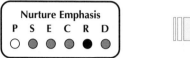

The Place: A force field analysis helps participants rationally assess important components of a challenging issue. It is a practice that is useful to individuals and groups when analyzing complex problems or decisions (Lewin, 1951).

The Process:

1. Identify the goal that is the focus of the analysis (e.g., creating a new position, implementing a program, improving achievement or results).

2. Provide a model for the force field analysis.

3. Identify forces that restrain or support goal resolution or achievement and mark each (e.g., with "x") to denote the extent of its influence.

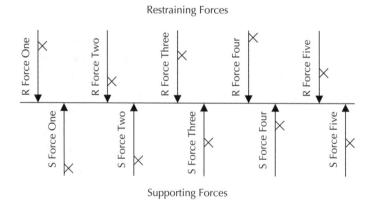

4. When the force field is complete, analyze how important restraining and support forces might be acted on to advance goal achievement.

The Payoff: A force field analysis mediates emotional reaction to challenging issues and tasks by structuring an objective assessment of what warrants attention. When conducted in groups, it socially pools and refines collective knowledge while promoting analytic thinking skills and dispositions important to problem resolution and decision making.

The Practice: RIP.10. Inductive Reasoning

The Place: Inductive reasoning is always at work in problem solving as the brain hypothesizes possible explanations and solutions from available information. It is useful to formally structure this practice, however, when individuals or groups are attempting to resolve complex problems.

The Process: Inductive reasoning puts information together to reach a probable conclusion. It is a process of inferring an explanation or a generalization from observation and other information. It is observed in the diagnostic work of doctors and the investigative work of detectives, reporters, and scientists. It is at work whenever the brain is putting information together to interpret something for which there is not an immediate or explicit explanation. The basic steps and a graphic for the process follow.

1. Observation of a phenomenon or problem for which there is not an immediate explanation or answer (e.g., apathy toward new initiatives).

2. Collection of relevant information (e.g., what are people saying or doing? How are they involved? What initiatives have been proposed? How many? How often? How were they developed? How were they introduced? Were they implemented, assessed, and successful?).

3. Examination of patterns or relationships within relevant information.

4. Construction of a probable explanation or hypothesis based on information patterns and relationships (e.g., people are apathetic about new initiatives because they are not fully involved in their formulation and, therefore, have little sense of ownership or commitment).

5. Collecting further information that will test the tentative explanation (e.g., (a) communicate with staff regarding how they are involved and might be more effectively involved in organizational planning and

development and (b) pilot alternative approaches for directly involving staff in the investigation and discovery phase of action planning).

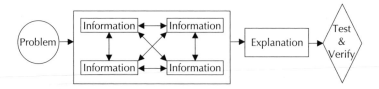

The Payoff: Inductive reasoning compels an emotional (and preferably social) focus on the assembly of refined knowledge to enable reflective inference. It is a methodical disposition and approach for constructing a best guess.

The Practice: RIP.11. Systems Analysis

The Place: Systems analysis is a means to see the forest and the trees. It is a formal approach to understanding the pieces and relationships that form the whole of an organization, program, procedure, object, or organism. As such, it is a practice that is useful to both individuals and groups when engaged in system planning, problem solving, or decision making.

The Process: Systems analysis helps the brain see patterns within the big picture that might be manipulated to greater advantage. Initially, it focuses on system components and relationships. It then projects alternatives for system improvement or transformation through attention to specific components. Steps and a graphic organizing the process follow:

1. Describe the parameters of the system to be analyzed. Virtually every system is composed of other systems and a component of a larger system (e.g., your body system is a collection of many biological systems and, in turn, a component of social, economic, and political systems). Thus, a systems analysis must establish the boundaries of the system to be explored (e.g., a staff development or learning system can be defined by the parameters of a department, district, or region).

2. Discuss the analysis purpose (e.g., periodic review, specific concern).

3. Create a graphic display that describes essential components in relationship to the focus system:

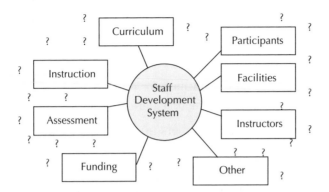

4. Raise questions and explore options around the identified components.
   a. What does this component contribute to the system?
   b. What are subcomponents of this component?
   c. What is working well regarding this component?
   d. What is not working well regarding this component?
   e. What additional information do we need about this component and where can we get it?
   f. How would the system be affected if we changed this component?
   g. What are our options?

5. Develop action plans for adjusting or changing system components.

The Payoff: A systems analysis is best done, of course, from the advantage of social interaction between system stakeholders. It is practice that structures emotional focus, refined knowledge, and complex reasoning. It also promotes analytic and creative thinking dispositions.

The Practice: RIP.12. ABVD Analysis

The Place: An ABVD (at, been, vision, do) activity structures problem analysis and decision making in a format that quickly accesses the collective wisdom of small or large groups. It moves participants through divergent reflections to convergent consensus about favorable solutions or actions. For that reason, it is useful in organizational planning and action research. The activity does not require excessive space but is best organized in meeting rooms that accommodate room for small groups (e.g., triads) to huddle and "think on their feet." It can also be adapted, moreover, to a sit-down version when applied to small groups or subgroups in more restricted spaces.

The Process:

1. A problem or issue is identified for analysis (e.g., a new technology, workplace safety, unsatisfactory performance, client concerns).

2. Triads are formed and members number themselves 1–3.

3. Each triad forms the following pattern on a section of open floor space using available artifacts (e.g., pencil, pen, notebook, can of soda) to mark the ABVD positions approximately three feet apart:

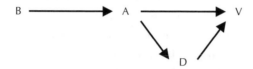

4. Triad members individually move through the ABVD sequence by standing at each position and responding to one of four questions related to the assigned issue. Each member moves through the sequence before the next member begins. Group members listen and take notes while others are moving through the positions within a prescribed time limit (e.g., 1–3 minutes per position):
   - Position A = What is the current state of the problem or issue? (i.e., where are we?)
   - Position B = What has/is contributing to the current state of the problem or issue? (i.e., where have we been?)
   - Position V = What is the vision of the preferred state of the issue or problem? (i.e., where should/could we be?)
   - Position D = What action(s) will move the problem or issue from the current state to the preferred state? (i.e., what will we do to get to where we want/need to be?)

5. After all group members have been through the ABVD sequence, each triad compares notes about observations expressed at each position and identifies consensus points and action recommendations.

6. Each triad reports on their consensus points and actions to the collective group according to the ABVD sequence.

7. The collective group discusses affinities within the triads' reports to further refine consensus points and action recommendations.

The Payoff: Participants in an ABVD process experience a very direct social interaction about an emotionally arousing issue or problem. That interaction refines related knowledge and taps the collective analytic and creative reasoning of a group. It also favors the dispositions of careful listening, open mindedness, questioning, and interdependent thinking.

The Practice: RIP.13. Storyboard

Nurture Emphasis
P S E C R D

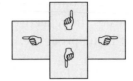

The Place: A storyboard is an approach to group problem solving that incorporates elements of problem clarification (i.e., RIP.16), brainstorming (i.e., RIP.3), affinity grouping (i.e., RIP.5), and consensus (RIP.7). It is also another example of progressive brainstorming (i.e., RIP.4). It is made distinct, however, by its emphasis on problem description and the physical manipulation of alternative solution scenarios.

The Process: A storyboard is fairly well defined by its name. It is a process of sequencing pieces of a story on "boards" of paper that are progressively reconfigured to discover revealing relationships and promising alternatives. Just as there are many ways to interpret a story, there are innumerable ways to employ storyboards in planning, problem solving, and decision making. One approach to formatting the process is

1. Describe the problem scenario (i.e., the story) that is to be analyzed and resolved and post it on a large card or sheet of paper.

2. Identify significant components of the problem (i.e., 3–5 significant pieces of the story) on cards below the posted problem.

3. Assign subgroups to brainstorm and post solutions on cards below the posted components.

4. Rotate the subgroups to enrich the pool of alternatives posted under each problem component.

5. Physically organize posted alternatives under the problem components by affinities and record prominent and thematic ideas on new cards.

6. Assess for commonalities in ideas across all the problem components and, if there are any, record them on new cards.

7. Remove all posted alternative cards and post the prominent idea cards.

8. Physically manipulate the prominent idea cards under the posted problem description to contemplate alternative "best solution" scenarios (e.g., one particularly promising course of action or a sequenced combination of several).

9. Record the consensus solution scenario and move to implementation.

The Payoff: A storyboard is an uncomplicated approach to exercising social interaction toward the reflective compounding of ideas. It also promotes the dispositions of being proactive, open-minded, analytic, and creative.

The Practice: RIP.14. Position Construction

The Place: A position construction is a means for bridging the constructive and reflective capacities of the brain. It is particularly useful when individuals and groups are confronted with controversial issues or challenging decisions and there is need to reference a credible knowledge base.

The Process: The process of a position construction is one of building support for an opinion, decision, or proposed action. It is a process that occurs at many levels in the brain's everyday business of rationalizing options (e.g., justifying the cars we purchase, the beverage we drink, or the career we pursue). In a more formal mode, position construction is a matter of organizing and communicating a convincing rationale to boards, colleagues, and clients. It then necessarily articulates a position supported by reasoned facts, examples, traditions, and authoritative sources. A graphic structure for organizing such construction is as follows:

Position: (e.g., a decision or opinion related to a topic, problem, or program)			
Reason:	Reason:	Reason:	Reason:
Factual information that supports the position	Examples that support the position	Established practices, traditions, or values that support the position	Authorities that support the position
Postconstruction reviews and updates			

The Payoff: A position construction assumes an emotional motivation to resolve a compelling decision or problem. That given, the exercise structures the direct and indirect social engagement of other brains in constructing refined knowledge and reviewing supportable options. It is a practice that is very encouraging of the dispositions of being accurate, organized, questioning, and analytic.

The Practice: RIP.15. Position Critique

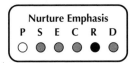

The Place: A position critique is the obvious close cousin of a position construction, as it also bridges the constructive and reflective capacities of the brain. In this practice, however, the goal is to test the positions constructed by self and others for flaws and errors. It is a particularly useful means by which individuals and groups can verify the integrity of arguments and opinions associated with controversial issues or challenging decisions.

The Process: The conduct of a position critique is analogous to that of a building inspector in that a construction is being inspected for possible flaws in supporting structures and materials. To that end, the process of a position critique examines the reasoned facts, examples, traditions, and authoritative sources assembled in support of a position—and offers assessment of the construction strengths and weaknesses. A graphic structure for organizing such a critique is as follows:

Position: (e.g., a decision or opinion related to a topic, problem, or program)			
Reason:	Reason:	Reason:	Reason:
Factual information that supports the position	Examples that support the position	Established practices, traditions, or values that support the position	Authorities that support the position
Critique of the position by assessment of supporting facts, examples, traditions, and authoritative sources – including recommendations and/or counter argument			

The Payoff: A position critique protects against flawed or pernicious arguments. It structures social and emotional attention to the quality of knowledge underlying personal positions and the positions of others. It is encouraging of the dispositions of being accurate, organized, questioning, and analytic.

Practices That Challenge Thinking

The brain is facilitated in its reflective chores by structures that focus its natural capacities. Reflection is a capacity, moreover, that can be pushed. Indeed, the brain revels in the opportunity to strut its best stuff—to tackle the difficult problem and create what is imagined. Examples of such practices that challenge the brain follow.

The Practice: RIP.16. Problem Clarification

The Place: Problem clarification promotes understanding about the parameters of a problem. Organizations are challenged to resolve many issues and conflicts. Clarity about the essential nature of a complex problem informs the judicious allocation of time and energy prior to resolution efforts.

The Process: Problem clarification is a process of bringing into sharper focus questions or other matters of uncertainty or difficulty. It is generally what de Bono (1996, p. 70) terms a "problem finding" process. For example, a simple but powerful approach is for an individual or group to repeatedly complete the sentence stem "The problem is . . ." regarding a topic or issue of concern. In generating a succession of different perspectives and interpretations of the nature of the problem, the participant(s) progressively flesh out the dimensions of the problem—and what is most important to attend to. A more formal format for that process follows:

1. Identify a topic or issue of concern.

2. Use a chart to brainstorm what the problem is and is not (see example on pg. 161).

3. With reference to the insights generated in step 2, describe the essential nature of the "real problem" as it is now understood.

The Payoff: Clarification of the character of a problem sorts out what is consequential to the task at hand. The process also promotes the refinement of relevant knowledge and the dispositions of questioning and seeking

The problem is . . .	The problem is not . . .
1.	1.
2.	2.
3.	3.
4.	4.
5.	5.
The real problem is:	

clarity. When conducted in groups, a collective intelligence further focuses the problem.

The Practice: RIP.17. Rational Clarification

The Place: The motivation behind an assertion, position, decision, or practice is not always what it might first appear to be. A rational-clarification exercise structures the examination of underlying concerns—the root causes and compelling values that influence action or a stand on an issue.

The Process: The process of rationale clarification arises from the traditions of dialogue and questioning long employed in philosophy to promote analytic reasoning. Costa (2001) describes Socratic questioning as representative of this prompting of critical reflection. The general idea is to follow the statement of a claim or assertion with a series of questions: Why is this true? What sources of information support your reasoning? What are the implications of your position? What assumptions are you making? What further assumptions arise from those assumptions? What are alternative ways to explain this? The structuring of the process, moreover, should not be complicated. Fogarty (2002) and Caroselli (2002) are among the students of the tradition who describe practical applications. A simple example is that of posing a succession of five "why" questions:

1. An initial claim or assertion is followed by the question, Why?

2. The response to the "why" prompt is followed by the question, Why?

3. The response to the "why" prompt is followed by the question, Why?

4. The response to the "why" prompt is followed by the question, Why?

5. The response to the "why" prompt is followed by the question, Why?

The Pay-off: The process of rationale clarification structures social and emotional analysis of knowledge and beliefs associated with a topic or issue. It progressively leads reflective thought beyond the surface to discover deeper understanding and motivation. It also exercises the dispositions of being clear, questioning, analytic, and intellectually honest.

The Practice: RIP.18. Analysis of Perspective

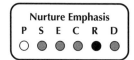

The Place: Analysis of perspective is a means to push the brain beyond its initial understanding of an issue. It is a useful practice for extending group knowledge and reflection about controversial problems and decisions.

The Process: There are many approaches to exploring alternative perspectives of an issue. The following procedure captures the essential steps of the process:

1. Participants extend their right arm in front of them at chest level with the palm facing down in a fist and thumb extended to the side.

2. A controversial issue is identified (e.g., charter schools, universal health care, a pending school referendum).

3. Participants indicate their position (i.e., for or against) by rotating the thumb of their fisted hand up or down (they may reflect for a moment, but they must signal a thumb-up or thumb-down position on the issue).

4. Participants lower their arms and write down their rationale, that is, the reasons behind their position on the issue.

5. Participants write down what they believe advocates of the opposing position would compose as a rationale for their position.

6. Participants pair with someone who has assumed the opposite position (i.e., a thumb up with a thumb down).

7. The paired participants take turns sharing the rationale they have prepared for their position. They do not question or respond to the rationale of the other person; they just listen and take notes.

8. After listening to each other's rationales, the paired participants compare what their partner said in defense of his or her position to what they predicted they might say (i.e., step 5).

9. Individually, in pairs, and/or as a larger group, participants discuss the relative merits of shared information and revisit their original positions and rationales (i.e., steps 3 and 4) to contemplate adjustments.

The Payoff: An analysis of perspective exercise proactively protects the brain against the "double bind" of its knowledge-construction proclivity. That is, it encourages the brain to entertain information that it is inclined to dismiss due to preexisting patterns of thought. The process also structures social and emotional comfort for reviewing difficult issues. The dispositions of being open-minded, questioning, and analytic are also encouraged.

The Practice: RIP.19. Perspective Scan

The Place: A perspective scan is a means to obtain multiple perspectives of an issue before decisions are made and action taken. It is a useful practice when an individual or group faces particularly challenging decisions.

The Process: The essence of a perspective scan is the solicitation of multiple points of view to generate deeper understanding of an issue and related options. It can be structured many ways, but the general idea is to see the issue from as many perspectives as possible. Moving the brain through a 360-degree review of an issue is useful to that end.

1. Clarify the issue to be explored (e.g., a program implementation, personnel decision, resource allocation, new technology).

2. Have one person represent the issue and sit in the center of a circle.

3. Have other participants sit in a circle around the "issue." They can either represent themselves or role-play other stakeholders/authorities.

4. The person in the center takes notes as multiple perspectives of the issue are shared by the outer circle.

5. An alternative approach would be to progressively turn the hub of the circle to different points (e.g., six to eight) of the outer circle representing specific stakeholders or authorities. At each stop, everyone in the outer circle offers a perspective of the problem from that point.

6. The notes recorded at the center of the circle are consolidated and reviewed for prominent themes and ideas.

The Payoff: A perspective scan reduces the prospects of overlooking knowledge or opportunity. A social review of an issue from many vantage points refines knowledge while generating understanding of viable options. It also promotes the dispositions of careful listening and questioning, as well as the inclinations to be open-minded, analytic, and creative.

The Practice: RIP.20. Reflective Role-Play

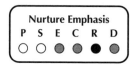

The Place: A reflective role-play is a variation of the role-play practice described in Chapter 6 (i.e., CIP.18). As such, it is an effective vehicle for constructing and communicating refined knowledge. It is a practice made more analytic, moreover, when employed by individuals or groups for the purpose of generating alternative perspectives of complex issues.

The Process: A reflective role-play involves more than assuming the role of a specific individual for the purpose of acquiring associated knowledge. The process here is to apply the perspective of the embodied individual to the problem or issue at hand. The idea is to see through the eyes of someone else—to imagine, as von Oech (1990) advised, how others would see and respond to the issue given their world view and experience. The intent is not to just become acquainted with the wisdom of Eleanor Roosevelt or Stephen Hawking; rather, such roles are taken on to provoke alternative insights. Thus, a reflective role-play might be structured as follows:

1. Establish the problem or issue to be analyzed and discussed.

2. Assign the role(s) and determine a preparation/presentation schedule.

3. Access relevant information and otherwise prepare the role-play.

4. Play the roles in an invented environment (perhaps a radio or television talk show or an international panel) to create a reality context for the famous or not so famous figures to share their expertise, perspectives, and recommendations about the targeted issue.

5. Debrief the role-play for insights gained and questions that remain.

The Payoff: A reflective role-play is a very social experience that fosters the emotional dissonance necessary to new insight and creative imagination. Most important, the responsibilities of a reflective role-play encourage the reflective interplay of thesis, antithesis, and synthesis. The practice also encourages the dispositions of being open-minded and analytic.

The Practice: RIP.21. Debate

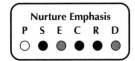 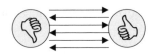

The Place: A debate is a powerful reflective tool for ensuring that controversial issues are fully explored and understood prior to important decisions being made.

The Process: The process of debate is in play anytime two or more people are contesting ideas or actions. The general idea is to construct support and analyze errors for conflicting positions on a specific issue. In that sense, debate shares the attributes of position construction (RIP.14) and position critique (RIP.15). A defining difference, however, is the depth of social interaction associated with debate. Although debates often occur between two individuals, the impact of the practice is further magnified when structured as a collaborative exercise. The following example, as adapted from a controversy activity developed by Johnson and Johnson (2002), describes the basic process of debate, as well as how collaboration can be incorporated to realize greater effect:

1. Identify an issue about which there are definable positions (two or more) that are in conflict (e.g., pro/con on prayer in public schools).

2. Form teams (e.g., two or three) to represent the opposing positions (e.g., Team A and Team B).

3. Teams prepare arguments for their assigned positions on the issue.

4. Teams present, listen, and note arguments for the assigned positions.

5. Teams counter each other's arguments, pointing out errors and flaws.

6. Teams reverse positions (i.e., Team A now becomes Team B and Team B becomes Team A) and—referencing their notes from the prior presentations and counter arguments—prepare improved arguments for the position they had previously opposed.

7. Teams present and counter improved arguments for reversed positions.

8. Teams drop positions and engage in whole group discussion of the compelling arguments and supportive evidence presented in steps 4–7.

9. The group explores a consensus position on the debated issue.

The Payoff: Any debate activity is going to provoke focused social interaction and emotional attention in the construction and critiquing of informed positions on an issue. When a collaborative structure is integrated, the impact of the practice on the refinement of knowledge and the dispositions to socially listen, question, analyze, and share is compounded.

The Practice: RIP.22. Reverse Perspective

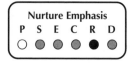

The Place: A reverse-perspective exercise forces the brain out of entrenched patterns and approaches. It is useful to both individuals and groups as a means to generate insights and options when confronting challenging issues.

The Process: The process of a reverse perspective can be formatted in a variety of ways to serve a variety of objectives. The basic idea, nevertheless, as elaborated on by von Oech (1990), de Bono (1996), Michalko (1998), and others, is to adopt a 180-degree reversal in how one perceives or approaches an issue or process. This is, in effect, what climbers do when they plan their assault strategies and supplies backward from the top of the mountain. It is also at work when architects delay the location of concrete walkways on campuses until students show the way with the paths they blaze on grass. Another form of this process is a simple reversal of the usual approach toward resolving a problem:

1. Identify a goal (e.g., improved productivity, reduced stress, better communication, efficient program implementation).

2. Reverse the goal (i.e., what you wanted to improve you now want to worsen, and what you wanted to reduce you now want to increase).

3. Generate ideas about how the reversed goal might be achieved.

4. Identify the most potent ideas for achieving the reversed goal.

5. Reverse back to the original goal and, with reference to step 4, contemplate what is most important to do to achieve that goal.

The Payoff: Looking in a different direction is a simple approach to seeing things differently or seeing things not seen before. A reverse perspective facilitates that phenomenon by confronting the brain with the extreme opposite of the desired result, which quickly focuses what is most important to attend to. It also has an immediate impact on emotional arousal to the task and—particularly when conducted in groups—the disposition to be creative.

The Practice: RIP.23. Deep Thoughts

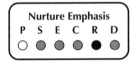

The Place: Deep thoughts about what is most important to attend to are there for the thinking anytime an individual or group is so disposed. They are periodically useful for sorting out serious concerns from thoughts that are distracting.

The Process: Deep thoughts about priorities and values emerge from deep questions that strike at the heart of things. "Trigger interview" questions described by van der Heijden (1994, pp. 279–281) offer a good example of how such deep reflection might be provoked:

1. What two questions would you most like to ask an oracle?

2. What is a good scenario for you right now?

3. What is a bad scenario for you right now?

4. What would have been a useful scenario to foresee 10 years ago? What did you think was going to happen then?

5. What are the most important decisions you face right now?

6. What constraints do you feel on making those decisions?

7. What do you want on your epitaph?

The Payoff: A deep-thoughts exercise helps to emotionally and socially center individuals and groups on a compelling purpose. Accordingly, it orients further analysis of important knowledge and options. It is a practice that promotes the dispositions of being introspective and analytic.

The Practice: RIP.24. Provocative Projection

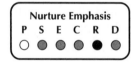

If...

The Place: A provocative projection is useful when it is important to consider possibilities either neglected or feared. It is a practice that is employable in both individual and group planning.

The Process: A provocative projection is basically a process of posing what van Oech (1990) labeled "what if" questions about issues or topics. As such, it is a quick and easy scenario process that gets the reflective juices flowing. A few examples follow.

1. What if the consolidation of schools into larger systems was reversed?

2. What if federal and state bureaucracies were reduced by 50%?

3. What if critical and creative thinking was the priority of every school?

4. What if all health and education services were home based?

5. What if technology makes education as we now know it obsolete?

The purpose of a provocative projection in any case is not to predict the future. Rather, the idea is to anticipate what could happen and the implications thereof. For that reason, the concern is not to critique the likelihood of the "what if" (although you do not want to spend your time contemplating flying pigs). The intent is to escape the ruts of complacency and contemplate what is imaginable, and thereby possible (e.g., as a terrorist attack in the United States and global recession and environmental warming was imaginable in 1990).

The Payoff: A provocative projection triggers emotional focus and the reflective manipulation of information to explore possibilities. It naturally promotes the dispositions of open-mindedness and creative and analytic thinking.

The Practice: RIP.25. Scenario Planning

The Place: Scenario planning asks the question, If this were to happen in the future, what would we do today? It is a practice that Royal Dutch/Shell Group used to anticipate oil shortages and *glasnost* in the previous century (Senge, Kleiner, Roberts, Ross, & Smith, 1994)—and an exercise that too few people applied to their investment portfolios at the turn of this century. It is a powerful means for shaking up one's worldview and fully engaging the reflective capacities of groups in planning and decision making.

The Process: Scenario planning is a process of imagining—rather than predicting—what could happen in the future. The intent is to raise awareness and sensitivity about what is happening in the present. It is a process of exploring phenomena and making distinctions that the conventional wisdom ignores. A basic format and graphic for the process is

1. Clarify the purpose for the scenario exercise by connecting it to a genuine and compelling concern that all participants share (e.g., what careers should we be preparing students for? What knowledge, skill, and character is essential to the success of this organization over the next 10 years? How will people obtain information, communicate, and learn in the future?). The idea is to move past concerns people think they have to what really matters and is truly motivating.

2. Review predetermined forces (e.g., the predictable number of 18-year-olds entering the work force in a region or nation in 2020) and uncertain forces (e.g., how many people will move to New

Zealand or become vegetarians) that will or might be in play in the future (this is the beginning of the imagining).

3. Describe several scenario plots—stories that will pull participants past their blindness to events and circumstances that could occur. (e.g., military service and training becomes the postsecondary education option of choice for most high school graduates, the birth-rate declines by 25%, a combination of technology advances and home and charter school options reduce public school enrollments by 50%, world terrorism doesn't go away, China completes a full transformation to democratic capitalism, scientific breakthroughs produce dramatic reductions in disease and increases in food supplies). Again, the purpose is not to predict what is likely or unlikely; rather, the idea is to entertain a story that is plausible and illuminating.

4. Discuss strategy. Given the stories laid out in each of several scenario plots, what would it be like to live in such worlds? What strategies would be effective in each? What strategies would be universally relevant to all the scenarios?

5. Review implications. Is there anything we need or want to reconsider or address regarding our present course of action based on this scenario exercise?

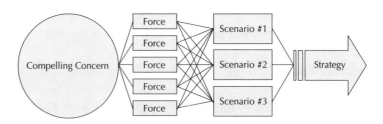

The Payoff: Scenario planning helps the brain take on the future between the eyes, rather than being blindsided in the temple. It structures a socially compelling and emotionally motivating reflection about complex relationships and patterns. It is also an exemplary exercise for promoting the dispositions of being proactive, open-minded, analytic, and creative.

The Practice: RIP.26. Metaphor

Leadership

The Place: Question: What's a metaphor? Answer: Grazing cows. After you have finished moaning, you might consider how that simple joke offers insight about how metaphor serves reflective thinking. That is, metaphor—like the punch line of a joke—has the effect of helping the brain see things it wasn't looking for. Thus, metaphor usefully stimulates creative insights that benefit understanding and problem resolution.

The Process: The process of metaphor is one of making linguistic comparisons that transfer qualities between dissimilar objects. Thus metaphor is commonly employed as a means to explore new avenues of thought or to provoke insight and fresh ideas. For example, an educator might metaphorically reflect, "curriculum, instruction, and assessment are like juggling because. . . ." Another example would be a health professional reflecting that "the current state of health insurance is like a pothole because. . . ." Given the observations generated by such reflection, participants have constructed more patterns to work with as they subsequently explore their options. The good news is that there are many ways to invite metaphor to your reflective processes: For example,

1. Open a book or magazine to a random page and randomly point to a word and then examine how that word represents a problem or issue of concern to you.

2. Go for a walk, look out the window, or gaze around the room and identify a random object or two or three to employ in metaphorical comparisons to your issue or problem.

3. Look to nature. The creations and workings of nature are primary metaphorical sources of inspiration.

The Payoff: Metaphor is an example of how the reflective brain can assert its executive function to manage the rest of the brain to advantage. In other words, it is an example of how the brain can direct itself to first creatively think about an issue and then determine how to best act.

The Practice: RIP.27. Invention

Nurture Emphasis					
P	S	E	C	R	D
○	●	●	●	●	●

The Place: Invention is a means to apply the imaginative powers of the brain to the creation of original products and processes. It can be proactively engaged by individuals and groups in any context that is receptive to improvement.

The Process: Invention is a process of creating a new or improved product or process. It is a process that calls upon the brain's capacity for imagination, ingenuity, and experimentation to satisfy perceived needs. As such, it is a pervasive exercise in human life as individuals and groups aspire to create an original idea, new strategy, or better mousetrap. It is a thinking process associated with the creation of technologies, theories, policies, systems, music, literature, and art. The primary components of the process are

1. Identify a need or opportunity for a new/improved product or process.

2. Describe the attributes of the product or process that will fulfill the identified need or opportunity.

3. Design, develop, and refine the product or process according to the described attributes.

The Payoff: The key point to be made about invention, perhaps, is that its applicability to immediate needs and opportunities is often overlooked. Is there any need for a new or improved product or procedure in your organization? Invention is not something that is reserved for the Wright brothers or Thomas Edison or the people at NASA. It is a process that takes the bridle off the mind and lets it roam—to pursue its best and most emotionally motivating work. It is a disposition well worth nurturing.

The Practice: RIP.28. Focus Forum

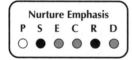

The Place: All groups necessarily organize their resources to a desired effect. Whether in the form of a football huddle or a strategic plan for a major corporation, there is a natural need for involved members to communicate and plan so that their collective efforts are effectively coordinated, so that they are on the same page and working toward the same goal. A focus forum is a means to structure such communication and planning at all levels (e.g., large systems or specific sites, departments, or work teams) and is adaptable to one or multiple-day time frames.

The Process: A focus forum is an approach to answering the fundamental planning questions any group aspiring to a common purpose must answer: (1) Who are we? (2) Where are we? (3) Where are we going? (4) How will we get there? (5) How will we know we are there? Those questions form the core of all organizational planning formats, whatever their label (e.g., strategic planning as described by Mintzberg, 1994). As such, this process focuses the big picture and is generally more demanding of facilitator time and expertise than other practices described in this book—particularly when applied to large systems. For that reason, facilitator training in this or similar formats is recommended through workshops and/or shadowing opportunities. It is also a process that incorporates or accommodates most of the other 100 approaches to engaging human capacity described in these chapters. That said, an example of a focus forum process as adapted from approaches described by Mintzberg (1994), Weisbord and Janoff (1995), and others is as follows.

1. A brief orientation (i.e., what will happen when and how).

2. A focus on the external context
   a. What is the current state (i.e., global, national, regional, local)?
   b. What are the projected states?
      i. What is the probable future?
      ii. What is the preferred future?
   c. What are the salient themes about the probable/preferred future?

3. A focus on the system
   a. Hindsight (i.e., where the system has been—its history)
   b. Insight (i.e., where the system is at—its preset state of strength and need)
   c. Foresight (i.e., best/worst case scenarios)

4. A focus on the future
   a. What goals will stretch us toward the preferred system and future?
   b. What strategies will advance the system toward its goals?
   c. What policies will guide strategy implementation?

5. A focus on compelling purpose. Note: There are different schools of thought as to whether this component should be addressed initially, intermittently, or at the end of a focus forum exercise. It is placed at the end of this example as it might if the group wanted to draw and test their true sense of their values and mission from their prior focus on context, system, and future (i.e., a form of a RIP.22 reverse-perspective exercise).

a. What are our values (i.e., what are the fundamental, shared beliefs that will support our collective efforts to adhere to policies, implement strategies, and achieve goals)?

b. What is our mission (i.e., what is our compelling purpose)?

The Payoff: The old expression, "every wind is a fair wind for the sailor without a destination" captures the purpose and payoff of a focus forum. It is a practice that comprehensively captures the collective capacity of an organization for reflective problem solving and decision making in planning. In the process, it cultivates a wide range of productive habits of thinking and collaboration.

The Practice: RIP.29. Action Forum

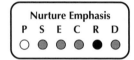

The Place: An action forum is the logical and necessary next step following a focus forum. As the name implies, the purpose of this practice is to act on the strategies and goals identified in the focus forum because—as we all well know – it is action that makes the difference.

The Process: Action forums are organized many ways and go by many names. Indeed, several of the practices previously described (e.g., SIP.10 action planning, EIP.10 future set, EIP.13 climate check, RIP.11 system analysis, RIP.12 ABVD analysis, RIP.13 storyboard) demonstrate all or most of the elements of an action forum. What would make an action forum somewhat distinct, nevertheless, is that it might be formally organized as an extension of a focus forum. The process in any case is one of

1. Review the system plan produced by a focus forum.
   a. Values
   b. Mission
   c. Goals
   d. Strategies
   e. Policies

2. Identify an action focus.
   a. Which goal(s) do we wish to act on?
   b. Which strategy will focus our action?

3. Plan the action(s).
   a. What is the specific objective?
   b. What are options for achieving the objective?
   c. Which option will we enact?
   d. How will we act on it (i.e., what are the details of the plan)?

4. Document the action plan(s).

5. Assign management responsibilities for the plan.

6. Implement the plan(s).

7. Record and report plan result(s).

The Payoff: Planning and implementing action toward the achievement of clear goals is the way productive things happen in an organization. This activity occurs incidentally all the time, of course, as individuals and groups go about their normal business. An action forum formally leverages the power of cooperation and collective intelligence in such planning. It is a process that connects brains around a compelling purpose, pools knowledge, and focuses the forces of analytic and creative thinking. Many productive dispositions are inevitably nurtured in the process.

The Practice: RIP.30. Assessment Forum

The Place: Assuming that there are definite goals to be achieved (e.g., either preexisting or produced by some version of a RIP.28 focus forum) and that there are structured attempts to act on those goals (e.g., through some version of a RIP.29 action forum), it is wise and necessary to know if and how actions are affecting progress toward goals. An assessment forum serves this purpose in instances of formal organizational planning.

The Process: An action forum follows the natural problem-solving sequence of identifying a goal and alternative options for its resolution, applying a promising alternative, and observing the result. This process is necessarily attached to any action-planning format (e.g., SIP.10 action planning, EIP.10 future set, EIP.13 climate check, RIP.11 systems analysis, RIP.12 ABVD analysis, RIP.13 storyboard, RIP.29 action forum). It is more formally structured to accommodate periodic (e.g., quarterly or annual) assessments of progress made toward system goals as follows.

1. Review the system plan produced by a focus forum.
   a. Values
   b. Mission
   c. Goals
   d. Strategies
   e. Policies

2. Assess plan progress.
   a. What strategic actions were conducted and what were the results of those actions (i.e., a summary of actions planned, executed, assessed, and reported through RIP.29 action forums)?
   b. What progress has been made on plan goals as measured by standards and benchmarks?

3. Report plan progress to stakeholders

The Payoff: A focus on clear goals and the planning and execution of plans for achieving represent the requisite first two legs of the planning triangle. Assessment is the obvious and essential third piece. It is assessment that provides invaluable emotional and analytic leverage on the brain when worthy goals are in view. The brain is oriented by compelling purpose, and it is motivated to do its best work by observable progress in resolving meaningful challenges.

Reader Reflection

With reference to the preceding story, this section provides an opportunity for reflection about the related knowledge constructions that are occurring in your brain about the nature and nurture of reflective capacity. To that end, the template that follows on the next page will facilitate a reflective response to three questions.

1. What do you now know about the reflective nature of intelligence?

2. What does this knowledge mean to you (i.e., what are the most important insights, conclusions, or implications that emerge from what you know)?

3. What action(s) will you pursue given what you know and judge to be important?

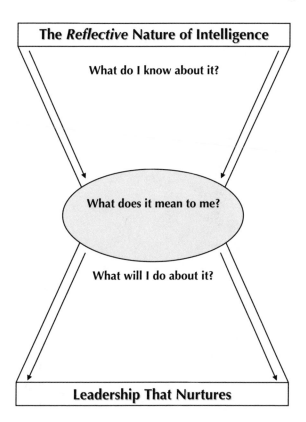

8

Dispositional Nature and Nurture

The Story of Dispositional Capacity

Maxine's brain has habits. It is disposed to mental tendencies that either productively maximize or detrimentally minimize the exercise of intelligence. The story of Maxine's dispositional brain, then, is an account of why and how the brain habitually exercises multidimensional capacities for thinking and learning. It is also a story about the value productive habits of mind bring to the human experience.

The Way We Are

Nature versus nurture is dead. Long live nature via nurture.

—Ridley (2003, p. 280)

There are three qualities that define the dispositional nature of Maxine's brain. Specifically, her brain is (1) endowed with an extraordinary capacity for thinking and learning, (2) programmed to automatically exercise that capacity, and (3) discretionary in how well it exercises such capacity.

This is all good news—with a qualifier. It is Maxine's good fortune that she has been gifted by nature with an extraordinary capacity that is available on demand and according to how she chooses to engage it. Therein lies the rub, however, as capacity does not ensure effective utilization or realization of potential. Natural capacity to walk, talk, or create visual images does not automatically evolve to ballet, opera, or the Mona Lisa. Likewise, human capacity for intelligence, regardless of how programmed and automatic it is, does not necessarily translate into intelligent behavior.

Dispositions are habitual behavior patterns that are rooted in genetic blueprints but malleable by experience. Variously referred to as habits, tendencies, inclinations, attitudes, personality, character, or temperament, they are observable in every arena of human activity. They serve as behavior templates that affect hygiene, exercise, diet, interpersonal relations, work, and virtually any other activity that presents an option of how to act. In fact, it is difficult to imagine human existence without the element of habitual behavior. Life would be considerably more difficult to manage on a moment-to-moment basis if Maxine had to continually pause to reflect about each and every behavior option. The establishment of habitual behavior patterns relieves her brain of such mundane preoccupation about how to act in every instance (e.g., to be positive or negative, open-minded or closed-minded, etc.). The trick, of course, is to establish productive dispositions that generally guide advantageous behavior over the wide range of human activity, thus freeing the reflective powers of her brain for more momentous tasks.

Notably, Maxine is genetically disposed to exercise physiological, social, emotional, constructive, and reflective dimensions of intelligence. There is no choice in this matter. It is her human nature to acquire, organize, and apply information in such fashion. It is as natural as breathing. To be human is to habitually engage the

- *Physiological nature* of brain capacity for monitoring and processing information through a biological platform of cells, circuits, and chemicals that is intimately integrated with the entire physiology of the body
- *Social nature* of brain capacity for interacting with other brains to learn and achieve
- *Emotional nature* of brain capacity for arousing mind and body to advantageous responses and actions
- *Constructive nature* of brain capacity for the discernment, organization, and storing of useful information patterns from the richness of environmental experience
- *Reflective nature* of brain capacity for consciously assessing objectives, obstacles, and options
- *Dispositional nature* of brain capacity for organizing broad patterns of thinking and behavior that are perceived to be of some survival advantage

Returning once again to the primary business of Maxine's brain, her dispositions can be interpreted as habitual patterns of behavior that the brain at some level—consciously, or subconsciously, disposed by nature or nurture or a combination thereof—judges to be of survival value. This does not mean that a particular behavioral pattern is indeed a good one; it just means her brain at some level believes that it is somehow useful to behave in a certain manner (e.g., to be habitually positive or negative, open- or closed-minded, timid or adventurous, trusting or suspicious, active or lethargic). Such dispositions evolve from the electrochemical compositions, allocations, and interactions that mediate all human behavior. That is, dispositions are ultimately the product of electrochemical activity within the neural networks of Maxine's brain. Some are factory installed in her brain by virtue of the genetic endowment of the human species as passed on from her parents. This is why, as a child, Maxine was naturally disposed to construct understanding by forming hypotheses, making predictions, conducting experiments, and formulating theories about how people, things, and language work (Gopnik, Meltzoff, & Kuhl, 1999). Dispositions originally installed, however, are subsequently and continually malleable by the influence of environmental experience. Thus Maxine's brain is disposed to certain habits of mind by both nature and nurture. The potential quality, of course, lies in the nurture.

Maxine's multidimensional capacity for learning and achievement must be consciously and regularly exercised if it is to realize its potential. Accordingly, her disposition to *consciously* exercise specific capacities is key to maximizing her intelligence. The question then is, what might such disposition look like if applied broadly to different dimensions of the nature of human intelligence?

The Way We Might Be

To be or not to be, that is the question.

—Shakespeare (*Hamlet*, Act III, scene i)

Shakespeare's Danish prince might make a compelling case for the option to exist or not exist, but if he is to be, he has no option other than to adopt dispositions of thought and behavior. As Dewey (1933, p. 89) advised, "mental habits, whether good or bad, are certain to be formed." Accordingly, if one is to be, the next question is how one will be.

Maxine came into this world equipped and disposed to engage multiple intelligence capacities. She is also disposed by nature to adopt standardized responses to stimuli as an alternative to having to constantly make moment-to-moment decisions about how to respond to her environment. The value of this refined dispositional exercise of intelligence rests on its contribution to survival. For example, a survival difference is made in Maxine's brain by virtue of opting to be persistent, creative, open-minded, organized, and analytical as opposed to uncommitted, traditional, closed-minded, random, and unquestioning. Incredibly, beyond this natural and necessary affinity for adopting dispositions of thought and behavior, Maxine's brain—by virtue of its reflective capacity—can exercise the additional option of adopting a disposition about her dispositions. That is, she can consciously attend to what condition her disposition is in. Significantly, it is her disposition to consciously assess and engage intelligence that holds sway over all other human potential.

What, then, might Maxine do if she is to be all she might be? Beyond her natural disposition to exercise her brain-enabled intelligence lies the opportunity to employ specific strategies that maximize the phenomenon. This perception is reflected in the observations of a wide range of scholarship about effective thinking and specific qualities of effective thinkers. Notably, scholars in this arena argue for the distinction between human capacity for intelligence and specific thinking strategies that take full advantage of said capacity. Examples of habits attributed to effective thinkers include Covey's (1989) conclusion that highly effective people are proactive, look to the end, put first things first, seek first to understand, then be understood, seek win-win solutions, synergize, and sharpen the saw (i.e., continually pursue self-renewal in the physical, social-emotional, mental, and spiritual domains). Similarly, Costa and Kallick (2000) have described 16 habits of mind displayed by intelligent people in response to problems, dilemmas, and enigmas (i.e., persisting, managing impulsivity, listening with understanding and empathy, thinking flexibly, thinking about thinking [metacognition], striving for accuracy, questioning and posing problems, applying past knowledge to new problems, thinking and communicating with clarity and precision, gathering data with all senses, creating and innovating, responding with wonderment and awe, taking responsible risks, finding humor, thinking interdependently, and remaining open to continuous learning). Perkins (1995) and Marzano and Pickering (1997) have also identified qualities of effective thinking. Senge (1990) extends the discernment of such qualities to learning organizations characterized by attention to systems thinking, personal mastery, mental models, shared vision, and team learning.

It really does not matter which list of potent thinking habits Maxine might subscribe to, as long as it includes credible strategies for exercising the resources of intelligence. More important is that she thinks about her thinking and what kind of thinking she would benefit from doing more of. To that end, she would reflect from time to time about what productive thinking might look like if oriented to the very nature of her capacity to think. For example,

- A disposition to optimally exercise the *physiological dimension* of intelligence might be expressed through propensities for physical exercise, healthy diet, water consumption, fresh air, natural light, novelty, and stimulating environments.
- A disposition to optimally exercise the *social dimension* of intelligence might be expressed through characteristic propensities for seeking opportunities for interaction, collaboration, and the sharing and challenging of ideas.
- A disposition to optimally exercise the *emotional dimension* of intelligence might be expressed through characteristic propensities for mediating emotion in a manner that contributes to the quality of one's life (i.e., emotional intelligence), proactive management of detrimental stress factors, and orientation to compelling professional and personal purpose.
- A disposition to optimally exercise the *constructive dimension* of intelligence might be expressed through characteristic propensities for constructing personal understanding through direct sensory information experiences such as writing, speaking, drawing, enactment, assembly, experimentation, or demonstration.

- A disposition to optimally exercise the *reflective dimension* of intelligence might be expressed through characteristic propensities for engaging specific thinking strategies associated with planning, analysis, problem solving, decision making, conflict resolution, and creativity.
- A disposition to optimally exercise the *dispositional dimension* of intelligence might be expressed through characteristic propensities for metacognition (thinking about one's thinking) as it pertains to other dimensions of intelligence (i.e., physiological, social, emotional, constructive, and reflective).

Maxine is well advised to attend to her thinking. Perkins (1995), Sternberg (1996), Langer (1997), and Tishman (2000) are among those who have observed that, to a considerable extent, people can learn to think and act more intelligently—that good thinkers are made, not born. How important is the dispositional dimension of intelligence? Simply put, it is disposition that holds sway over all other dimensions of Maxine's intelligence. It is the arena in which her capacity to learn and achieve is either advanced or diminished.

The Meaning of the Story

The way we think is not the way we think we think.

—Fauconnier and Turner (2002, p. v)

Maxine's brain is disposed to conduct its business in ways that are both prescribed by nature and subject to nurture. Without such disposition, her brain would be hopelessly bogged down in overload and indecision. What, then, is most important for a leader to know and be guided by regarding the dispositional nature of the brain? Examples follow as to what might be worth knowing for the leader who is interested in the cultivation of productive habits of mind.

Macro

The brain adopts patterns of thinking—mental tendencies or inclinations— that are habitually applied on a broad scale as the brain conducts its survival business. The human brain interprets and organizes useful information patterns on all levels of scale. Thinking dispositions are products of the brain's pattern making at a macro level. They are neural constructions designed to process broad categories of environmental experience.

Mandatory

The brain has no option other than to develop and exercise habits of thinking—but there are options as to the quality of the habits targeted and developed. Every healthy human brain is genetically and environmentally disposed to the broad physiological, social, emotional, constructive, and reflective exercise of intelligence. The instinctive and habitual application of such capacities is essential to the brain's survival business. Furthermore, habits of mind are intended means for efficiently allocating the neural resources of the brain.

Malleable

Thinking dispositions are genetically introduced and environmentally influenced. Beyond basic genetic prescriptions, the human disposition to exercise intelligence to greater or lesser effect is malleable. That is, productive habits of mind are subject to the influence of physical environment, culture, and conscious reflection throughout the lifespan.

Maximizing and Minimizing

Thinking habits are determining factors in how far and well one travels the neural byways of the brain. Human capacity to think, learn, and achieve is realized to the degree that there is a productive disposition driving it. Sustained states of dispositional intelligence are defining elements of individual and organizational character. They are the means by which the potential of intelligence is explored and realized. Indeed, thinking dispositions are primary influences over the exercise and development of all other dimensions of intelligence (e.g., physiological, social, emotional, constructive, and reflective).

The Rest of the Story

Maxine's story is the final account in a series describing six dimensions of human capacity for learning and achievement. It is a story, nonetheless, that will be considered first and foremost by leaders who are serious about influencing individual and organizational capacity for the achievement of goals. Indeed, Maxine's story conjures up the classic wisdom about teaching a man how to fish so that he might feed himself for a lifetime versus giving a man a fish to feed him for a day. If thinking dispositions are mandatory yet malleable influences on how well the brain exercises its multidimensional intelligence, a leader is well advised to focus on the cultivation of productive habits of mind. Following, then, is the rest of the story—what might be done to nurture productive dispositions that habitually exercise and feed the mind.

Mindful Strategy

With reference to the dispositional nature of Maxine's brain, what might a leader do to nurture such capacity in self and others? Two suggested strategies follow.

Strategy: Exercise the Brain

Productive habits of mind do not just happen. The brain is disposed to employ a way of thinking to the degree that it has experienced it. Ergo, exercise the brain broadly.

Strategy: Target Productive Thinking Habits

Effective thinkers have productive thinking habits—habits that maximize their capacity to learn and achieve. Target and practice the habits that matter most.

Mindful Practice

This final story about the multidimensional brain ends with description of practices a leader might employ to nurture the dispositional nature of Maxine's capacity for learning and achievement. As has been the case in the prior chapters, the practices are aligned to strategies that (1) exercise the brain and (2) target productive thinking habits. The practices presented are also coded by an assessment of their primary (black), secondary (gray), and associated (white) influence on the physiological (P), social (S), emotional (E), constructive (C), reflective (R), or dispositional (D) nature of intelligence. The practices offered are again only examples intended to encourage a leader's inclination to employ at least 50 ways to nurture the dispositional dimension of brain capacity.

Practices That Exercise The Brain

The brain is endowed by nature with powerful and multidimensional means by which it conducts its intelligence business. That endowment must be exercised and conditioned, however, if its potential is to be fully realized. To that end, the 95 previously described practices are worth the exercise—both for their immediate effect on the brain and for the conditioning effect that leads to habituation. That is, if it is a good practice for productively engaging the brain, it is a practice worth doing, doing well, and doing until it is habitual. Five more practices follow that are particularly worth habitually exercise.

The Practice: DIP.1. Reflective Writing

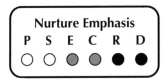

The Place: Reflective writing is a practical approach to cultivating a productive thinking disposition. The practice structures individual think-time in quiet, comfortable environments when there is opportunity for reflection about a topic or issue. It is an activity that is assignable in groups, but it can be conducted individually as well. It is also receptive to soft instrumental music as background.

The Practice: Reflective writing is obviously something that can be done with a minimum of effort and planning. It is also a favored practice of many of the "great thinkers" of history. The process can be further structured, however, beyond personal journaling as follows:

1. If an individual or group is new to the process, some preliminary orientation and sharing of reflective writing experience is advisable (e.g., free-writing, keeping a journal).

2. Select a catalyst for reflection about a particular topic or event:
   a. A related inspirational reading
   b. Exploration of emotional response
   c. Discernment of essential elements or qualities
   d. Interpretation of implications
   e. A stem sentence
   f. A summary review

3. Supply writing materials that are pleasant and inviting to use.

4. Provide ample time and space for writing in a quiet atmosphere.

5. If conducting the activity in groups, encourage sharing of individual reflections after the allotted writing time ends, while also assuring confidentiality for that which individuals want to keep private.

The Payoff: Reflective writing is an approach by which individuals and members of groups access their capacity for reasoning and thinking for themselves. As much as the brain expects and depends on social interaction to do its work, it also requires time to individually sort things out and put things together. Reflective writing provides an opportunity for thinking deeply about issues and exploring ideas. It encourages knowledge construction and the exercise of analytic and creative thinking. The reflective writing process also honors individuality, while sharing insights encourages the social scaffolding of ideas.

The Practice: DIP.2. Comprehensive Review

```
┌─────────────────────────┐
│     Nurture Emphasis     │    (*•} (*•} (*•} (*•}
│   P   S   E   C   R   D  │
│   ○   ●   ●   ●   ●   ●  │
└─────────────────────────┘
```

The Place: A comprehensive review is a mental exercise that wraps the multidimensional capacities of the brain around a significant problem or decision. It is, quite simply, one of the most proactive and mind engaging practices that an individual or group might habitually apply to their work.

The Process: A highly respected version of a comprehensive review is de Bono's (1985) *Six Thinking Hats.* That particular format uses the metaphor of putting on a variety of "thinking hats" when confronted with a challenging issue. The essence of the process in any format (e.g., hats, lenses, frames, cubes, or modes), however, is a systematic application of multiple dimensions of intelligence to the analysis of a specific question or problem. A generic approach might be formatted as follows:

1. *Emotional Analysis.* This analysis explores how the individual or group feels about issue at hand. The point is not to judge or explain or defend, but rather to acknowledge the emotion that is in motion.

2. *Constructive analysis.* This analysis focuses on an objective review of the facts of the matter—what is known and not known and what further information is needed and how to get it.

3. *Reflective Analysis.* Given prior assessment of emotional states and factual knowledge, this analysis is organized by three questions that collectively project merits, pitfalls, and options:

    a. What positive opportunities and possibilities reside within the issue under review? That is, what good could be realized in the form of improvements, new directions, or positive change(s)?

    b. What negative experiences lurk within the issue under review? What might go wrong, create a problem, or cause worry and woe?

    c. What are some alternative, new, or creative ways to approach and understand the issue under review?

4. *Dispositional Analysis.* This analysis assesses the range and productivity of thinking dispositions applied to the review process, that is, how well the emotional, constructive, and reflective analyses were carried out. Simply put, this is a matter of asking, How well did I/we think through this issue and how might I/we do better next time?

The Payoff: A comprehensive review brings the full range of the brain's intelligence capacities to a task in an overt and focused fashion. When habitually utilized, it is an exemplary approach to cultivating the dispositions of emotional intelligence, objectivity, and analytic and creative thinking.

The Practice: DIP.3. Sage Counsel

The Place: Sage counsel structures reflection with respected minds about important matters. It is employed to review events and options related to specific issues or general practices. It is useful when difficult decisions and problems call for good advice from self and other credible sources.

The Practice: The sage-counsel process organizes a conversation between oneself and others who have something to offer to the reflective needs of your brain. It is a process that can be conducted in one's head, as a role-play, or with reality participants. The steps in the process are as follows:

1. Determine the focus of the review (e.g., a pending career decision, a difficult personnel issue, a controversial program proposal).

2. Select a council of sage counselors. This can be done by organizing a council—either in your head or on paper using the graphic

below—composed of individuals whom you hold in high regard (e.g., friends, family, colleagues, mentors, historical figures, contemporary leaders). It can also be organized physically by subgroups within a larger group.

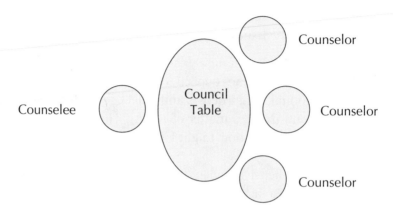

Counselor

Counselee

Council Table

Counselor

Counselor

3. Seat yourself in the counselee chair at the council table and conduct a conversation with your invited sage counselors seated around the table across from you. You can structure the conversation as you wish. It might be a formal inquisition or a simple chat over coffee. The point is to imagine and respond to questions or advise that your sage counsel might put forward.

4. If conducting the process physically with real people, the same process applies. If it serves your purpose, however, the participants might rotate and take turns being counseled.

The Payoff: Sage counsel is a deeply social reflection activity, even when imagined in one's head. It brings forth the emotional references and reflective dissonance associated with serious dialogue with wise people about meaningful issues.

The Practice: DIP.4. Thinking Space

Nurture Emphasis
P   S   E   C   R   D

The Place: A thinking space might be an empty beach or an isolated mountain trail. It might also be a quiet table with a glass of wine and pen and paper. It could as easily be a crowded room full of conversation. Whatever the context, a thinking space is a place where one goes to think.

The Process: The process associated with a thinking space is to have as little process as possible. Scheduling regular thinking appointments with an open beach, hidden trail, or quiet restaurant fills that requirement. The idea is to regularly go somewhere for the expressed purpose of thinking. This can also be done in groups as the examples of open-space meetings and bean suppers demonstrate. The concept of an open-space meeting is commonly credited to Harrison Owen (1997), though he is the first to acknowledge the natural human instincts that underlie the idea. It is an idea that originated from Owen's observation that meaningful conversations most often occurred over coffee outside of the meetings that people had originally assembled for. Working from that insight, he developed a meeting format that was purposefully left to the structuring interests of the participants. The guidelines for such meetings are (1) whoever comes are the right people, (2) whatever happens is the only thing that could happen, (3) whenever it starts is the right time, and (4) whenever it's over it's over. With those broad parameters, participants gather in an "open space" and (1) proceed to consider a focusing theme for the event, (2) review the guidelines for an open space meeting, (3) post and group topics of interest, (4) locate a convenient space for whoever is interested in like topics to gather in and converse as they wish, and (5) reconvene and share at the end of the event if and how they wish to do so. A bean supper is even less structured. This idea is attributed to the Mayo Clinic in Rochester, Minnesota, during its formative years (Senge, Kleiner, Roberts, Ross, & Smith, 1994) when clinic staff would regularly gather for potluck suppers in a large room on the clinic grounds. When simply gathered in that fashion over food, their conversations naturally gravitated to meaningful conversations about their work.

The Payoff: Just giving the brain space to think can be a powerful means to activate and sharpen reflective instincts, and the more often the space is visited, the more habituated and complimented the thinking becomes.

The Practice: DIP.5. Coaching

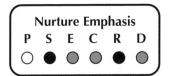

The Place: Coaching is a practice that helps others master knowledge, skills, or qualities of character. We perhaps best know coaching from observing it in sports activities and the performing arts. It can be specific to the mastery of specific knowledge (e.g., CIP.20), but it is also applicable to the honing of more refined applications of mind.

The Process: Coaching is a process of observing, listening, demonstrating, imparting knowledge, and providing feedback. It is what teachers do. When targeting good thinking habits, a coaching relationship with a colleague or other able individual is the equivalent of having a personal trainer for the mind. The success of such activity, moreover, is strongly influenced by the following criteria for quality coaching and feedback:

1. There is clarity about the targeted thinking skill (e.g., creative thinking, being more open-minded).

2. The coach is knowledgeable about the targeted thinking and able to model and offer examples that are immediately useful.

3. Feedback is descriptive rather than evaluative, specific rather than general, and directed toward behavior the receiver can adapt.

4. Coaching is available regularly and at the earliest opportunity after the targeted thinking behavior is observed.

The Payoff: We seek out coaches and trainers when attempting marathons, weight loss, and golf. Why not coach the mind to better habits? The likely bonus is that the coaching will be as productive for the coach as the coached.

A Practice That Targets Productive Habits

One develops good thinking habits by exercising good thinking. If a leader aspires to nurture the capacity of an organization, he or she will broadly facilitate the multidimensional exercise of intelligence in self and others. A leader will also target specific thinking practices for habituation (e.g., any one of the hundred previously described here) based on judgments of individual and organizational need. Once targeted, however, the dispositional practice that will determine the habituation of all others is practice.

The Practice: DIP.6. Practice, Practice, Practice

Nurture Emphasis

P	S	E	C	R	D
●	●	●	●	●	●

The Place: Anytime, all the time. There can be no confusion about *the* practice that determines whether individuals or groups will acquire and benefit from productive dispositions of mind. The practice to employ to acquire good thinking habits is to practice good thinking.

The Process: The process for the practice of exercising productive mental habits is to practice (i.e., habitually exercise) productive mental habits. There really is nothing more to say about this—except that the other hundred brain-friendly practices described in these chapters are good candidates to consider for your exercise regimen.

The Payoff: The endowment of a healthy brain is a gift. The exercise of productive thinking dispositions is what compounds the gift. In an organization, such development is an invaluable determiner of a productive culture.

Reader Reflection

With reference to the preceding story, this section provides an opportunity for reflection about the related knowledge constructions that are occurring in your brain about the nature and nurture of dispositional capacity. To that end, the template that follows will facilitate a reflective response to three questions:

1. What do you now know about the dispositional nature of intelligence?

2. What does this knowledge mean to you (i.e., what are the most important insights, conclusions, or implications that emerge from what you know)?

3. What action(s) will you pursue given what you know and judge to be important?

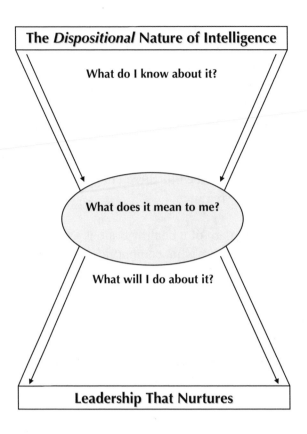

Part Three
Persistence

The mindful leader is attentive to the nature and nurture of intelligence in the process of influencing others to achieve goals. Moreover, such attention is not a momentary or incidental connection. A leader who is truly mindful of the nature of human capacity will persistently nurture that capacity in self and others. Over time, such attention holds promise for fostering a culture that collectively attends to organizational intelligence—a capacity-connected culture that maximizes learning and the achievement of purpose.

9

The Connected Culture

One can even hope that eventually practices of organizational intelligence will reach a point at which enough individuals and groups know and do such things that it becomes very awkward not to know and do them, and pretty soon most everyone will.

—Perkins (2003, p. 250)

Inform, Perform, Transform

This final chapter projects leadership that has made the leap to an emerging paradigm through perception, performance, and persistence. It is a projection of *mindful leadership* that is attentive to the nature and nurture of intelligence in the process of influencing others toward the achievement of goals (Dickmann & Stanford-Blair, 2002). More specifically, it describes *leadership that is connected in both perception and practice to human capacity for learning and achievement.* It is a projection that envisions how breakthrough knowledge about intelligence might *inform* how leaders *perform* to *transform* organizational culture. This projection is staged through five scenarios to portray a "big picture" of leadership influence on the building of a capacity-connected culture—a culture that maximizes a collective capacity for achievement.

The Connected Leader Revisited

The more complex society gets, the more sophisticated leadership must become.

—Fullan (2001, p. ix)

The connected leader is *mindful* of goals that matter and what it takes to achieve them—and then does something about it. Such a leader moves beyond the perception of compelling purpose, required capacity, and compatible behavior. Such a leader proceeds to employ practices that influence the capacities required to achieve the purpose. This mindful alignment of leadership influence to capacity and purpose necessarily begins with a worthy end in mind.

Knowing What Matters

For, in the end, it is impossible to have a great life unless it is a meaningful life. And it is very difficult to have a meaningful life without meaningful work.

—Collins (2001, p. 210)

If you are a mindful leader, you know what matters. You are consciously connected to what is important. The following scenario will help make this point. After reading the brief narrative, you are invited to visit the reflection zone that follows to discover your adeptness at discerning what is important.

Scenario 1: A Matter of Purpose

The radio alarm performed it duty as programmed at 6:00 A.M., but Nick was ahead of that cue by at least an hour. He had not yet emerged from under the quilt, however, choosing to review the pending day from the comfort of a prone position. He was pumped and ready. It was a good feeling.

The presentation was going to be a pivotal event, but Nick was only a bit nervous at this point in the game. The long hours of preparation had been productive, and he was confident that he and his colleagues had all their ducks in a row. The project was going to happen, and it was going to make a significant contribution. Looking back, however, Nick had to admit that he was both amazed and proud that things had progressed so well —despite the significant obstacles that had arisen along the way.

What had sustained the momentum of the project during those many moments of challenge and uncertainty? Was it simply a matter of people doing their job and collecting a paycheck—or was it the sense of important purpose that had started the group off on this journey? Was it some of both? What motivated people, for that matter, to take on and stick to any daunting task?

Nick continued to ponder those questions as he left the warmth of his bed. Whatever the answers might be, he was sure of one thing. He knew he was looking forward to the events of the day.

Reflection Zone

What is the compelling organizational mission or professional purpose that arouses and sustains your commitment (i.e., What gets you out of bed in the morning)?

_____

_____

What is an important job-related goal that you are presently working on?

_____

_____

The above reflection should make the point that you know what matters. It is not difficult for you to identify what is important to you personally and what motivates your professional commitment and effort. Similarly, you likely can bridge your personal motivation to the mission and goals of the organization you are affiliated with. You also know whether or not the passion is there. That is, if you struggled with the above reflection, you have reason to question your current career focus or affiliation.

Any leader who is productively connected to an organization knows what is important. Effective leaders know what compelling purpose motivates them and the people they work with. Indeed, leadership is necessarily centered by clarity of purpose. The power of emotional commitment is perhaps most apparent in love and war or in artistic or athletic performances, but it is a universal quality behind all human achievement. Indeed, lack of such orientation works to the disadvantage of individuals as well as groups—and inevitably diminishes leadership influence on organizational success.

Knowing What It Takes

What other reason for our superiority can we conjure up? We are neither the fastest nor the strongest of creatures. We're not even the most prolific . . . Thus, our minds constitute our sole claim to biology's throne.

—Vertosick (2002, p. 7)

The thoughts of a leader who is clear about purpose quickly turn to the human requirements of the task. The leader begins to connect to what he or she and others need to know, do, or be like to achieve goals related to a compelling mission. The question becomes, What will it take to get the job done? The following scenario and reflection zone focus on this leadership connection.

Scenario 2: A Matter of Capacity

Abigail sat at the desk and swiveled her chair to take in the expansive view offered by her new executive digs. She was still basking in the glow of her recent promotion to CEO of Better and Easier System Technologies. Her mind was rapidly shifting, however, from the emotional high of achieving a well-earned career goal. Reflective processes were coming on-line as she reviewed her new responsibilities.

Abigail had inherited a successful organization from her predecessor. A clear mission and sense of purpose had guided BEST in the achievement of organizational goals in recent years. She was aware, however, that there was no room for complacency in her business—you were either getting better at what you did, or you were losing ground.

Thus focused, Abigail pondered what BEST had to do to remain the best. The key, she knew, rested within the people whom BEST employed and retained. That much was obvious—an organization was only as good as its people. It was people who were willing and able to apply themselves to goals that made the difference.

Abigail realigned the chair to the desk and activated her computer. Her mind was zeroing in now. What did the members of BEST have to know, be able to do, or be like in order to perform and achieve well? She knew that the difference between success and failure would be more than a matter of specific knowledge or skill. There would always be new things to know and new skills to be acquired. What was required was something more fundamental and essential than the knowledge or skill of the moment. She stroked the keyboard as the conclusion emerged in her mind:

Organizational success will be increasingly determined by the capacity of all members to think and learn—both individually and together—in any situation that arises.

Staring at the screen, Abigail knew that this was not a unique insight. It was almost a "duh" observation. But her mind was moving on to the particulars of the issue. What is the bottom line? What kind of thinking and learning is most important? What is the fundamental nature of such capacity? What do I need to know and do about it?

Reflection Zone

What is important for the members of your organization to know, do, and be like?

_____

_____

What kind of thinking will be most important to your organization in the future?

_____

_____

What is the nature of human capacity for learning and achieving goals?

_____

_____

Similar to your discernment of compelling personal and organizational purpose, you are predictably adept at describing qualities of knowledge, skill, and character germane to such purpose. To get the job done, certain knowledge must be acquired, skills mastered, and character developed. Again, a leader who is viably connected to an organization would be expected to know this.

A broader assessment of human assets and needs is now possible, however, through reference to emerging knowledge about the nature of intelligence. Thus informed, a leader is oriented to the fundamental capacities for thinking and learning that will serve any goal or challenge that might arise. In this fashion, the leader's connection to human capacity becomes less situational and more foundational and comprehensive.

Herein lies the challenge to the leader who aspires to be more tightly connected to organizational capacity. *Beyond addressing what the members of the organization need to know, do, and be like in a given situation, a connected leader will also attend to the nature of intelligence that underlies the acquisition and application of all knowledge, skill, and character.* To that end, a leader will cultivate understanding about what matters most in all manner of human learning and achievement. He or she will understand that intelligence—the capacity to acquire and apply knowledge—operates in multiple dimensions in the brain:

The physiological dimension: the biological platform of cells, circuits, and chemicals upon which the brain's capacity for information processing operates

The social dimension: the capacity for social interaction that the brain expects to experience—and depends on—to do its job well

The emotional dimension: the capacity by which the brain is aroused to attention, makes judgments, and is motivated

The constructive dimension: the extraordinary brain capacity for perceiving, organizing, and remembering useful information patterns

The reflective dimension: the distinguishing brain capacity for consciously manipulating information—to review, analyze, project, rehearse, and create

The dispositional dimension: the brain capacity for mental tendencies that either productively maximize or detrimentally minimize the exercise of intelligence

To summarize to this point, a connected leader is mindful of compelling purpose and capacities for achieving that end. What remains is the action connection—how one might best act to bring potent capacity to bear on important purpose.

Doing Something About It

Strategies most often fail because they are not executed well. Things that are supposed to happen don't happen.

—Bossidy and Charan (2002, p. 15)

If you are in the leadership business, it is expected that you think about matters of purpose and capacity. Beyond *knowing* about what is important to do and what is required to do it, however, is the matter of *doing* something about it. It is action that determines success in the end. Accordingly, leaders who intend to make a difference move beyond perception to performance. They connect to actions that nurture capacities necessary to the achievement of purpose. The mindful leader knows that talk is cheap and action speaks louder than words.

Figuring out how to best nurture the capacity of others is, nevertheless, a challenging leadership task. The next scenario and reflection zone speak to this issue.

Scenario 3: A Matter of Nurture

"Welcome to the trenches," Chris thought to himself as he unpacked another box in his new office. He was already missing the formal preparation phase of his leadership journey. He had enjoyed the intellectual grappling with theory and research within the removed—and therefore safe—confines of the university classroom. That was not to say he wasn't looking forward to applying what he had learned to the real world. What good was knowledge if not applied to practical and purposeful ends? Nevertheless, Chris was understandably nervous about taking on his first formal leadership assignment.

He was more confident about some aspects of his pending responsibilities than others. He felt well prepared to work with others in developing clarity about the mission of the organization and then aligning related goals to that purpose. What he was less sure about was how to marshal human capacity toward the achievement of those goals.

Determining what members of the organization specifically needed to know, be able to do, and be like to achieve targeted goals did not intimidate Chris very much. He believed that it would be relatively easy to identify such needs through dialogue within the organization. He was more concerned about connecting to the fundamental capacities that underlie the acquisition and application of all knowledge, skill, and character. That was the more challenging part for a leader new to both the profession and the organization—knowing how to nurture such capacities in self and others.

"The devil is in the details," he reflected. "It isn't going to just happen by itself. To get the job done, I have to adopt specific strategies and practices— actions that will favorably influence organizational capacity for learning and achievement."

```
┌─────────────────────────────────────────────────────────────────────┐
│                         Reflection Zone                                │
│                                                                        │
│  What do leaders in your organization do to nurture learning and      │
│  achievement?                                                          │
│                                                                        │
│  _____        │
│                                                                        │
│                                                                        │
│  _____        │
│                                                                        │
│                                                                        │
│  _____        │
│                                                                        │
│  What should leaders in your organization do to nurture learning and  │
│  achievement?                                                          │
│                                                                        │
│  _____        │
│                                                                        │
│                                                                        │
│  _____        │
│                                                                        │
└─────────────────────────────────────────────────────────────────────┘
```

The alignment of leadership practice to clear purpose and perception of capacity might be a bit more difficult to pull off than one might first think. Indeed, it would appear that this is where many leaders stumble. How should one act to effectively influence others toward a desired result? This is a critical leadership challenge—one that many would-be leaders either fail to meet or, in the worst-case scenario, fail to even attempt.

Capacity-connected leaders act to influence others from their knowledge of how the brain works behind the scenes of human learning and achievement. Given a compelling goal orientation, the leader acts to influence others through specific strategies and practices. Most important, the strategies and practices employed are not randomly applied; rather, they are consciously aligned to the nurture of capacities deemed important to the achievement of goals. To that end, a capacity-connected leader might align a repertoire of strategies and practices around perceptions of intelligence as follows:

1. *Guiding perception about the physiological nature of intelligence:* The information-processing capacity of the brain is enabled by a biological platform of cells, circuits, and chemicals that are dependant on care received from the body.

Aligned strategy: Attend to brain fitness

Aligned practices:

PIP.1. Smart moves	PIP.2. Oxygen pumps
PIP.3. Waterworks	PIP.4. Music moods
PIP.5. Humor breaks	PIP.6. Neural buffets
PIP.7. Touching moments	PIP.8. Cohort aerobics
PIP.9. Fitness goals	

2. *Guiding perception about the physiological nature of intelligence:* Neural networks in the brain continue to grow and develop throughout the lifespan according to the quantity and quality of environmental experience encountered.

   Aligned strategy: Stimulate neural networks

   Aligned practices:

PIP.10. Network alerts	PIP.11. Mind-body development
PIP.12. Strange encounters	PIP.13. New ventures
PIP.14. Thought walks	PIP.15. Stimulating space

3. *Guiding perception about the social nature of intelligence:* When one brain meets another brain, the exercise of thinking and learning inevitably follows.

   Aligned strategy: Facilitate meetings of minds

   Aligned practices:

SIP.1. Brain waves	SIP.2. Dyad processing
SIP.3. Triad processing	SIP.4. Progressive processing
SIP.5. Basic jigsaw	SIP.6. Corner conversations

4. *Guiding perception about the social nature of intelligence:* The collective capacity of human intelligence is tapped when brains are enticed into collaborative relationships by clear, compelling, and mutually held goals.

   Aligned strategy: Cultivate common purpose

   Aligned practices:

SIP.7. Inspirations	SIP.8. Before/after action review
SIP.9. Base groups	SIP.10. Action planning groups

5. *Guiding perception about the social nature of intelligence:* The greater the diversity of experience and perspective in social interactions, the greater the prospects of strong and productive thinking.

   Aligned strategy: Extend the mind's reach

   Aligned practices:

SIP.11. Book groups	SIP.12. Mentor relations
SIP.13. Professional affiliations	SIP.14. Alien alliances
SIP.15. Technology adventures	

6. *Guiding perception about the emotional nature of intelligence:* The brain will not attend to other tasks if emotionally distracted by concerns for its physical or social welfare.
   Aligned strategy: Ease the mind
   Aligned practices:
   EIP.1. Group norms   EIP.2. Peer interviews
   EIP.3. Member checks   EIP.4. Victory laps
   EIP.5. Affirmations

7. *Guiding perception about the emotional nature of intelligence:* The brain is aroused and focused by emotional assessment of what merits attention.
   Aligned strategy: Excite the mind
   Aligned practices:
   EIP.6. Anticipatory set   EIP.7. Mission set
   EIP.8. Personal set   EIP.9. Reality set
   EIP.10. Future set

8. *Guiding perception about the emotional nature of intelligence:* The power of emotion must be managed to informational and motivational advantage by the rational capacity of the brain.
   Aligned strategy: Evaluate states of mind
   Aligned practices:
   EIP.11. Emotion check   EIP.12. Mood check
   EIP.13. Climate check   EIP.14. Parking lot meeting
   EIP.15. Conflict resolution

9. *Guiding perception about the constructive nature of intelligence:* The brain is motivated to construct meaning and memory about information that is emotionally and rationally valued.
   Aligned strategy: Justify construction
   Aligned practices:
   CIP.1. Preconstruction assessment   CIP.2. Construction review
   CIP.3. Construction mapping

10. *Guiding perception about the constructive nature of intelligence:* The neural construction of meaning and memory is influenced by social interaction and other rich environmental experiences.
    Aligned strategy: Facilitate construction
    Aligned practices:
    CIP.4. Sensory engagement   CIP.5. Construction pauses
    CIP.6. Construction notes   CIP.7. Graphic organizers
    CIP.8. Guiding questions   CIP.9. Knowledge expeditions

CIP.10. Reciprocal teaching   CIP.11. Reciprocal views
CIP.12. Memorization   CIP.13. Modeling
CIP.14. Practice

11. *Guiding perception about the constructive nature of intelligence:* Information patterns that are constructed and remembered will be continually refined by connections to new information—if the brain does not become too comfortable with existing patterns.
Aligned strategy: Extend construction
Aligned practices:
CIP.15. Knowledge updates   CIP.16. Comparison
CIP.17. Progressive jigsaw   CIP.18. Role-plays
CIP.19. Extended conversation   CIP.20. Extended coaching

12. *Guiding perception about the reflective nature of intelligence:* The reflective capacity of the brain is focused by thinking templates that apply to specific purposes, such as the thinking steps involved in problem solving, decision making, conflict resolution, invention, or inductive or deductive reasoning.
Aligned strategy: Structure thinking
Aligned practices:
RIP.1. Problem solving   RIP.2. Decision making
RIP.3. Brainstorming   RIP.4. Progressive brainstorming
RIP.5. Affinity grouping   RIP.6. Nominal group process
RIP.7. Consensus   RIP.8. Fish bowl
RIP.9. Force field analysis   RIP.10. Inductive reasoning
RIP.11. System analysis   RIP.12. ABVD analysis
RIP.13. Storyboard   RIP.14. Position construction
RIP.15. Position critique

13. *Guiding perception about the reflective nature of intelligence:* The essence of reflective reasoning is expressed in analytic and creative thinking.
Aligned strategy: Challenge thinking
Aligned practices:
RIP.16. Problem clarification   RIP.17. Rationale clarification
RIP.18. Analysis of perspective   RIP.19. Perspective scan
RIP.20. Reflective role-play   RIP.21. Debate
RIP.22. Reverse perspective   RIP.23. Deep thoughts
RIP.24. Provocative projection   RIP.25. Scenario planning
RIP.26. Metaphor   RIP.27. Invention
RIP.28. Focus forum   RIP.29. Action forum
RIP.30. Assessment forum

14. *Guiding perception about the dispositional nature of intelligence:* Productive habits of mind do not just happen. The brain is disposed to employ a way of thinking to the degree that it has experienced it.
    Aligned strategy: Exercise the brain
    Aligned practices:
    DIP.1. Reflective writing   DIP.2. Comprehensive review
    DIP.3. Sage counsel   DIP.4. Thinking space
    DIP.5. Coaching

15. *Guiding perception about the dispositional nature of intelligence:* Effective thinkers have productive thinking habits—ways of thinking that maximize their capacity to learn and achieve.
    Aligned strategy: Target productive habits
    Aligned practice: DIP.6. Practice, practice, practice

Because leadership is a process of influencing others to achieve a goal, a leader must necessarily connect to the three components of that process: the goal, the capacity of others, and actions that influence the capacity of others. This alignment of action to capacity and goals completes a capacity-connected leadership paradigm if—and this is the "big" if—the leader is mindful of the nature and nurture of intelligence in constructing such alignment. The narrative following Scenario 3 suggested how that alignment might be consciously attended to when a leader is committed to doing something about it. It is a portrayal of a leader who is connected to important goals, the nature of human capacity, and interventions that nurture that capacity toward goal achievement. The next sections project the potential effect of those leadership connections on organizational culture.

The Connected Culture

> *Ultimately, your leadership in a culture of change will be judged as effective or ineffective not by who you are as a leader, but by what leadership you produce in others.*
>
> —Fullan (2001, p. 137)

Culture is generally defined as the behaviors and beliefs characteristic of a particular group. It is a powerful force that both acclimates and guides group members in the conduct of their affairs. The power of culture as a blueprint for living is observed in the values, norms, language, myths, art, rites, and rituals of a group—elements that strongly orient members to what is important, what to do, and how to do it. Given the power of culture, Drucker

(1973), Schein (1991), Fullan (2001), and Senge, Kleiner, Roberts, Ross, and Smith (1994) are among the many who have encouraged leadership attention to its nature and nurture. It is advice based on the perception that leadership influence on others is most strongly realized through effect on organizational culture.

Cultures Norm

Why do so much education and training, management consulting, and business research and so many books and articles produce so little change in what managers and organizations actually do?

—Pfeffer & Sutton (2000, p. 1)

Just as individuals unavoidably adopt dispositions unique to themselves, organizational cultures necessarily develop defining characteristics. As is also true of the tendencies and inclinations cultivated in people, the qualities of culture that evolve and take root will inevitably be more or less productive in their effect. To get a better handle on the quality differences in organizational cultures, read the following scenario and then visit the reflection zone that follows.

Scenario 4: Qualities of Culture

Arriving at work, Amy reflected that she knew what it was like to win the lottery. She was beginning her third year with Actualized Health Associates (AHA) and loved her job. She loved everything about it—the people she worked with, the meaningful focus on preventative health care, and . . . and . . .

Amy became aware that her mind was faltering in its reflection about her job satisfaction. What was it, exactly, that made her feel so positive about being at AHA? She had the same basic responsibilities at AHA that she had in her previous job, a position that also focused on health care. What was it about AHA that was different? What made her feel so positive and productive and convinced that she was working in a much better place? She was mindful that her attitude about her current situation was almost a 180-degree reversal of her feelings about her professional experience immediately prior to joining AHA. She shuddered just thinking of it. Working at Dumas Units Ltd. (DUL) was a nightmare she would almost like to forget. Almost, because—unpleasant as it was—remembering DUL helped Amy to more fully appreciate AHA.

Because she was early for her shift, Amy decided to seize the moment and reflect further about what made the difference. Grabbing a pencil and a pad of paper, she began to note what distinguished AHA from DUL. What was it about AHA that made it such a great place to work, and what was it that made working at DUL so dissatisfying?

Reflection Zone

What are qualities of the ideal organization (i.e., what most favorably influences the productivity and satisfaction of the members of a group)?

_____

_____

_____

What are the qualities/characteristics of the organization from hell?

_____

_____

You know a good organizational culture when you meet one. Conversely, you can likely articulate the qualities of a group you would rather not be associated with. It is also safe to assume that your reflection identified significant disparities between your perceptions of the "ideal culture" and the "culture from hell." Given those assumptions, the good news is that the organizational culture is subject to environmental influence. That is, qualities of culture—whatever their degree of entrenchment and resistance—are malleable, both in what they evolve to be and what they might yet become. Difficult as it may be to achieve, you can have the culture you want.

Being aware that cultures form to norm the beliefs and behaviors of their members, there is an understandable human interest in discerning advantageous cultural qualities. Accordingly, there is no shortage of advice regarding the determining characteristics of effective organizations. In their classic study of successful American companies, Peters and Waterman (1982) identified principles associated with organizational success that included a bias for action and staying close to the customer. Cunningham and Gresso (1993) have described correlates of effective organizational cultures such as collegial relationships, access to quality information, broad participation, lifelong growth, individual empowerment, and sustained innovation. Synthesizing much of the research in the arena of educational reform, Dufour and Eaker (1998) proposed that professional learning communities are characterized by shared mission, vision, and values; collective inquiry; collaborative teams; action orientation and experimentation; continuous improvement; and results orientation. Collins' (2001) more recent investigation into exceptional organizational success advocated for, among other qualities, the importance of disciplined people, thought, and action. All such attempts at defining the essence of what makes the difference in the success of individuals and groups are in themselves characteristic of the nature of the human intellect—we want to figure it out. There is also the supposition within such inquiry that if we understand what makes the difference, we can marshal our resources to create those conditions.

Of late, there is a new twist in the quest for the culture that makes a positive difference. Emerging revelations from intelligence research and theory provide an unprecedented opportunity to align organizational cultures to the very essence of human nature. This idea is not new in itself. Senge (1990), Perkins (1992), Drucker (1992), and Fullan (1991) are but a few of the voices that have historically advocated for "learning organizations" that more fully appreciate and exercise the intelligence capacities of all members. What has changed, however, is that science has opened the door to a more direct approach. There is no longer a need to work at the edges of the issue. If nature has deemed it valuable to equip the human brain with survival advantages in the form of definable dimensions of intelligence, how might an organization hope to do better than to subscribe to what nature has ordained?

It is time for a more conscious alignment of organizational culture to what matters most to human progress and prospects. There is opportunity now to build organizational culture though perceptions and practices that are directly attuned to the physiological, social, emotional, constructive, reflective, and dispositional capacities that define human nature. If a culture is formed to norm beliefs and behaviors, would it not be best formed to norm an organizational value for understanding and exercising intelligence?

The door is open, and it is time for leaders to step through and engage new possibilities.

Cultures Transform

Once the players have mastered the system, a powerful group intelligence emerges that is greater than the coach's ideas or those of any individual on the team.

—Jackson (1995, p. 92)

If the character of the culture exerts a powerful influence on how members understand and behave in an organization, it is worth contemplating the character of an organizational culture defined by its orientation to the nature and nurture of intelligence. It is a reflection that merits attention because it projects a comprehensive and profound leadership influence on others. This last scenario and reflection zone address what that might look like—a " big picture" of an organizational culture in which being mindful of the nature and nurture of intelligence is "the way we do things around here."

Scenario 5: The Capacity-Connected Culture

Emily waited uneasily for the applause to subside behind the glare of the studio lights. The introduction was too effusive for her tastes—and a bit at odds with what she was about to talk about. She was nervous in any case. She was never completely comfortable with the medium of nationally televised talk shows, nor had Tom Prince interviewed her previously. Mindful of her elevated emotional state, she employed a favored mantra for calming her mind, silently affirming that "this is not about 'me.'" Thus focused, Emily locked on to her host's initial probe from across the table.

Tom: "Emily, we're most pleased to have you with us today. To get things started, why don't you share what it feels like to be the CEO of an organization selected by Smart Org. Magazine as one of the most innovative and improved organizations in the nation."

Emily: "It feels good. Remembering what it was like when we were less successful helps everyone at Binet Integrated Quality appreciate our present status."

Tom: "I'm thinking that we might as well cut to the chase here. I'm sure our viewers are most interested in knowing how you turned things around at BIQ.

Emily: "Well, a very important part of the answer to that question is that it was what *we* did to realize *our* success. I accept the responsibility that comes with any formal leadership position; however, the most important responsibility that I have as a leader is to fully involve everyone in the pursuit of organizational success. To the degree that I am successful in fulfilling that one task has everything to do with how successful the organization becomes."

Tom: "Point taken. But I do think you are being a bit modest. Just the fact that you value the importance of everyone's involvement would, it seems to me, have something to do with the character and success of BIQ."

Emily: "I accept that. Either a leader appreciates and engages the human assets available to the organization or she doesn't. It is difficult to imagine, however, how any leader in this day and age would fail to recognize that two heads generally enjoy an edge over the capacity of one—and that the collective capacity of many heads is the potent resource to be tapped."

Tom: "OK, given that a leader is a true believer in the importance of tapping the collective capacity of the organization, how does a leader go about doing that?"

Emily: "I can only tell you what we do at BIQ. Specifically, we do three things—if you don't mind, I'll ask your technician to put up the first slide" (see Figure 9.1).

Tom: "Sure."

Emily: "As indicated on the slide, we follow a simple but powerful approach to aligning our collective capacity. First and foremost, we strive to be clear about our overall purpose, as well as the more specific goals related to that purpose. This in itself is nothing new to the world of organizational leadership. Most leaders are familiar with the why and how of developing organizational vision, mission, and goals. What we might do a little bit differently, however, is we talk about our purpose and goals all the time. We never start a meeting without reference to

Figure 9.1 Organizational Alignment of the Nature and Nurture of Capacity to Purpose

---

BIQ Slide One: Aligning Capacity to Purpose

1. *Be clear about purpose*

2. *Understand the nature of capacity*

3. *Act to nurture capacity toward the achievement of purpose*

what the endgame is. We are constantly reviewing, discussing, and refining our consensus about what is worthy of our time and effort. We also frequently remind each other of Collins' (2001, p. 1) observation that 'good is the enemy of great.'"

Tom: "And you don't think most organizations do that?"

Emily: "I don't know. Leider (1997), Boleman and Deal (2000), and Fullan (2003) are among those who cite the importance of a higher calling and core values in infusing individuals and organizations with passion and purpose. Commitment to a common purpose, nevertheless, is challenging to pull off in the reality of complex organizations. I also know, from both personal experience and anecdotes shared by colleagues, that attention to mission and goals can easily become superficial and perfunctory in an organization. For those reasons, we work hard at targeting and focusing what is important to strive for. Our attitude is that if we can't get excited about what we are doing, we don't have our eye on the right ball. In such instances, we pause for a serious gut check about what motivates us to get out of bed in the morning."

Tom: "Given your attention to purpose, what about understanding capacity?"

Emily: "This second point might be what differentiates us most of all. Simply put, we strive to understand who we are."

Tom: "You're losing me there. What do you mean by 'understand who we are?'"

Emily: "I mean we make the effort to know the nature of human capacity for learning and achieving—what makes us tick."

Tom: "Tell me more."

Emily: "It's not complicated. Everyone at BIQ is supported in developing a foundation of knowledge about the nature of intelligence. We all have a practical understanding of what capacities lie under the hood—the potent forces that reside behind the eyes and above the ears of everyone in the organization."

Tom: "How does everyone at BIQ develop this knowledge?"

Emily: "Again, our approach is pretty simple. There are any number of ways one could go about organizing the large body of scientific information about the brain and the intelligence it enables. Our goal, however, is not to prepare people to be neuroscientists. Rather, our interest is that we all have a good base of understanding about how the brain does its best works and how we might best use it to our advantage. So, we had our HR department work up an introductory Intelligence 101 seminar that all employees—myself included—participate in as part of their initial orientation and training when they come on board at BIQ."

Tom: "What do people learn in this seminar?"

Emily: "We have organized the seminar content around six dimensions of intelligence that have been extensively researched across many fields of scientific inquiry. Our goal is to establish a foundation of essential knowledge about the physiological, social, emotional, constructive, reflective, and dispositional nature of intelligence."

Tom: "And that's it then? They know what they need to know?"

Emily: "Actually, it's just the beginning, albeit an important beginning. When people finish the seminar, they have processed knowledge about the role of physiology, social interaction, emotional management, sensory construction, structured reflection, and productive dispositions in learning and achievement. Of course, people already have a knowledge base about such content when they come to us. In that sense, the seminar serves to further refine and organize what they already know. Most important, the seminar promotes common knowledge and language for communicating about how we might best approach the work we do. The most interesting part of our intelligence learning, nevertheless, happens postseminar."

Tom: "How so?"

Emily: "Few things are of as much interest to the brain than information about itself. Once members have had the opportunity to learn together about what is going on inside their heads, they are inclined to continue the dialogue."

Tom: "So what do you do about that?"

Emily: "A variety of things. It can be as simple as informal study groups, book talks, dissemination of pertinent articles, or direction to relevant websites. We also arrange for workshops, speakers, and other more formal opportunities to apply our intelligence to the matter of intelligence. The point is, understanding human capacity is not a one-time shot at BIQ. Knowledge about how we learn and achieve continues to evolve, and we attend to new information as it is revealed."

Tom: "You mentioned earlier that your attention to the nature of capacity was perhaps a distinction between BIQ and other organizations. What do you mean by that?"

Emily: "Business as usual in some organizations might not be particularly attentive to how people best learn and achieve. This is worrisome, because the evidence suggests that such attention is essential to organizational success."

Tom: "Examples?"

Emily: "Take your pick. From Peters and Waterman (1982) and Deming (1988) to Collins (2001) and Bossidy and Charan (2002), numerous investigations of productive organizations have identified structures and processes that are consistent with what is now known about the physiological, social, emotional, constructive, reflective, and dispositional dimensions of human capacity. Recent studies more directly address intelligence-productivity connections. For example, the work of Goleman, Boyatzis, and McKee (2002) consolidates research findings about the powerful relationship between emotional intelligence and individual and group achievement."

Tom: "So, this new information might lead to improvements and greater efficiencies?"

Emily: "Right. Leaders have always known that the success of an organization is dependent on the qualities of its people. So they would intuitively work to tap into those qualities. That's why Jack Welch (2001) attributed GE's success to their creating the greatest people factory in the world. If we can now better understand how human intelligence works, we can better nurture it to advantage. We can better support the exercise of intelligence by self and others. We can promote more effective applications of intelligence across the organization."

Tom: "And that brings us to the third point on the slide?"

Emily: "Exactly. At BIQ we act to nurture capacity. This point recognizes that knowledge about the nature of capacity is prerequisite, but action provides necessary nurture. To that end, our attention to the nature of intelligence includes learning about strategies and practices that nurture it in individuals and groups."

Tom: "So it's a matter of knowing both the nature and nurture of intelligence."

Emily: "Yes, but the key to this last point is in the acting. There is a big difference in knowing how to act and actually doing it."

Tom: "I'm guessing you have a way to encourage such action."

Emily: "We have found that knowledge about the nature of intelligence is in itself a strong influence on how people subsequently behave at BIQ. This is a natural effect observed in the influence of new information in general. For example, when a brain constructs new understanding about its social bias in learning and achievement, it is disposed to apply that knowledge to future behavior."

Tom: "So, that's all you do?"

Emily: "No. We also systemically introduce and model practical practices that are aligned to specific dimensions of intelligence. In fact, as an organization, we have identified general strategies that are aligned to fundamental perceptions about the multidimensional nature of intelligence. We then organize compatible practices to the strategies. I think the second slide shows this" (see Figure 9.2).

Tom: "Yes, its going up now. But why this organization of strategies and practices?"

Emily: "The strategies and practices we employ are aligned to the nature of the capacities we intend to nurture. They are also based on research about interventions that most effectively influence learning and achievement as reported by Joyce and Showers (1982), Slavin (1990), Johnson and Johnson (2002), Marzano (2003), and many others. What is particularly compelling, by the way, is the vast research base that reports the positive influence of collaborative learning structures across the physiological, social, emotional, constructive, reflective, and dispositional dimensions of intelligence."

Figure 9.2   Attributes of a Capacity-Connected Organizational Culture

---

BIQ Slide Two: Attributes of the Capacity-Connected Culture

1. *Clarity About Goals*

2. *Common Perceptions About the Nature of Intelligence:*
    - *Intelligence operates on a biological platform of cells, circuits, and chemicals.*
    - *Social experience is the great provocateur of thinking and learning.*
    - *Emotion is the means by which the brain attends, judges, and is motivated.*
    - *The brain, as a biological system, is a lean, mean pattern-making machine.*
    - *The brain reflectively manipulates information and options prior to action.*
    - *Thinking dispositions either maximize or minimize the exercise of intelligence.*

3. *Aligned Strategies and Practices That Nurture Intelligence:*
    a. *Nurture the physiological platform that enables intelligence.*
        - *Attend to Brain Fitness 50+ ways*
        - *Stimulate Neural Networks 50+ ways*
    b. *Promote social relationships.*
        - *Facilitate Meetings of Minds 50+ ways*
        - *Cultivate Common Purpose 50+ ways*
        - *Extend The Mind's Reach 50+ ways*
    c. *Harness the power of emotion.*
        - *Ease the Mind 50+ ways*
        - *Excite the Mind 50+ ways*
        - *Evaluate States of Mind 50+ ways*
    d. *Facilitate the construction of meaning.*
        - *Justify Construction 50+ ways*
        - *Facilitate Construction 50+ ways*
        - *Extend Construction 50+ ways*
    e. *Build a culture of reflection.*
        - *Structure Thinking 50+ ways*
        - *Challenge Thinking 50+ ways*
    f. *Cultivate mindful dispositions.*
        - *Exercise the Brain 50+ ways*
        - *Target Productive Habits of Mind 50+ ways*

Tom: "There are preferred practices that everyone uses at BIQ?"

Emily: "Yes and no. The whole idea is that if a goal situation calls for social interaction or the construction of new knowledge or reflection, whoever is involved will have a repertoire of practices available to facilitate the required brainwork. There are, of course, some standard tried-and-true structures that are used often, such as in problem-solving and decision-making situations. But we also want to be careful not to curb our creative talents or opportunities to try new approaches. So we have adopted a 50 ways understanding about the practices that are used to facilitate thinking and learning in the organization. That understanding is that there are some good standard approaches available to be used. But there might be at least 50 other good ways to any approach. So, if you discover or think of another good way to facilitate social interactions in reflective problem solving, go for it."

Tom: "That brings up a question. What do you say to the critic who just doesn't buy what you're doing and how you're doing it, someone who honestly questions the value of attending to the nature and nurture of intelligence in organizations?"

Emily: "The short answer is, if you are a leader, you really don't have a choice in the matter. You unavoidably influence the capacity of the organization by how you behave in it. The only option is whether you are going to act in a manner that enhances or constrains that capacity. But hey! If you suspect the merits of attending to organizational intelligence, don't do it. If you doubt there is value in such attention, then just continue to influence the organization in a less informed, more intuitive fashion. Some leaders are very good at this intuitive approach. Indeed, historically leaders had no other option, given that scientific information about what went on inside of people's heads was not readily available. Given that we now have such information, BIQ and other organizations are deciding that knowledge is power—that there is advantage in being intelligence informed. The times call for greater intelligence, and we aspire to satisfy the need. Given that, there are undoubtedly other ways to go about this than the way we do it."

Tom: "So, what's the bottom line about the BIQ approach?"

Emily: "The second slide sums it up. We aspire to build an organizational culture that is tightly connected to our most important assets. We develop and sustain that culture through the systemic acquisition and application of knowledge about the nature and nurture of intelligence. It is a purposeful alignment that connects perceptions and practices that are important to the achievement of goals."

Tom: "And by systemic you mean . . . ?"

Emily: "Everyone is attentive to the same knowledge base as they go about their work throughout the organization. Over time, that systemic approach has generated a mindful culture that is attentive to the nature and nurture of intelligence in the pursuit of goals. I think the last slide presents that concept" (see Figure 9.3).

Tom: "It does, and that's also a good place to end it, given that our time is up. Thank you for visiting with us about BIQ and its capacity-connected culture."

Emily: "My pleasure."

Reflection Zone

What might a leader do to constrain organizational intelligence?

_____

_____

What should a leader do to promote organizational intelligence?

_____

Figure 9.3. The Cultivation of a Capacity-Connected Organizational Culture

BIQ Slide Three: The Development of a Capacity-Connected Culture

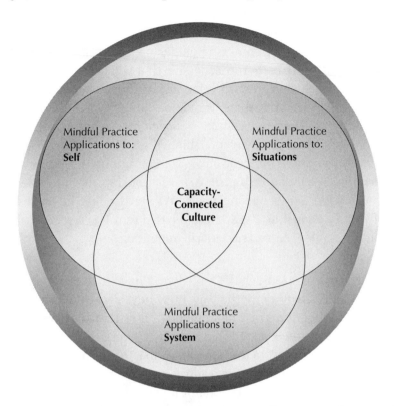

A "capacity-connected" organizational culture (i.e., a culture characterized by attention to the nature and nurture of intelligence in individuals and groups) emerges through systemic applications of practices that are mindful (i.e., attentive) of intelligence capacities in self, situations, and the system over time.

The Greater Connection

> *Very little in our lives is more important and more pervasive than our relationships with those we care about and with whom we work. And very little is more inscrutable and problematic. Relationships can be as taxing and toxic as they can be replenishing and fulfilling.*
>
> —Barth (2003, p. xi)

The human brain is wired to learn and achieve. Leaders need to understand and fully appreciate the nature of that capacity. More important, leaders need to know how they might more effectively influence such capacity toward the achievement of good and meaningful purpose. They need to develop this knowledge and skill at a time when relationships within the human family— as well as relationships between the human family and the rest of the planet—are in much need of leadership assistance. Moreover, leaders are compelled by the emerging context to gather up lessons from the leadership that has been and move on to the leadership that will be. Central to that new leadership will be a more refined relationship to the workings of human intelligence, both in self and others. Most important will be the need for leaders who can further advance our collective capacity for acquiring and applying information—the intelligence relationship within our social species that has brought us this far and is our only means for continuing the journey.

Leadership is a relationship. It is a relationship of influence on the capacity of others for achieving goals. We have many examples of the power of that relationship. We are also advised that it is a relationship that is continually challenged and necessarily renewed:

> I have walked that long walk to freedom. I have tried not to falter; I have made missteps along the way. But I have discovered the secret that after climbing a great hill, one only finds that there are many more hills to climb. I have taken a moment here to rest, to steal a view of the glorious vista that surrounds me, to look back on the distance I have come. But I can rest only for a moment, for with freedom come responsibilities, and I dare not linger, for my long walk is not yet ended. (Mandela, 1995, p. 751)

The leader's journey does not end. Leadership evolves to the next rise— and then steps forward again.

Reader Reflection

1. Where are you in your leadership journey?

2. In what ways do you already lead with the brain in mind?

3. How will you lead with the brain in mind in the future?

References

Aronson, E., Blaney, N., Stephan, C., Sikes, J., & Snapp, M. (1978). *The jigsaw classroom.* Beverly Hills, CA: Sage.

Barker, J. (1992). *Paradigms: The business of discovering the future.* New York: Harper-Collins.

Barth, R. S. (2003). *Lessons learned: Shaping relationships and the culture of the workplace.* Thousand Oaks, CA: Corwin Press.

Boleman, L. G., & Deals, T. E. (1991). *Reframing organizations.* San Francisco: Jossey-Bass

Boleman, L.G., & Deal, T. E. (2000). *Escape from cluelessness.* New York: AMACOM.

Bossidy, L., & Charan, R. (2002). Execution: The discipline of getting things done. New York: Crown Press.

Burns, J. M. (1978). *Leadership.* New York: Harper & Row.

Caine, R., & Caine, G. (1991). *Making connections: Teaching and the human brain.* Alexandria, VA: Association for Supervision and Curriculum Development.

Calvin, W. H. (1996). *How brains think: Evolving intelligence, then and now.* New York: Basic Books.

Calvin, W. H. (2002). *A brain for all seasons: Human evolution and abrupt climate change.* Chicago: University of Chicago Press.

Caroselli, M. (2002). *The big book of meeting games.* New York: McGraw-Hill.

Collins, J. (2001). *Good to great.* New York: HarperCollins.

Costa, A. L. (Ed.). (2001). *Developing minds: A resource book for teaching thinking.* Alexandria, VA: Association for Supervision and Curriculum Development.

Costa, A. L., & Kallick, B. (Eds.). (2000). *Discovering and exploring habits of mind.* Alexandria, VA: Association for Supervision and Curriculum Development.

Covey, S. R. (1989). *The seven habits of highly effective people: Restoring the character ethic.* New York: Simon & Schuster.

Cunningham, W. G., & Gresso, D. W. (1993). *Cultural leadership: The culture of excellence in education.* Needham Heights, MA: Allyn and Bacon

Damasio, A. (1999). *The feeling of what happens.* New York: Harcourt Brace.

de Bono, E. (1985). *Six thinking hats.* New York: Little, Brown.

de Bono, E. (1996). *Serious creativity: Using the power of lateral thinking to create new ideas.* London: HarperCollins Business.

Deming, W. E., & Walton, M. (1988). *Deming management method.* New York: Perigree.

Dennison, P. E., & Dennison, G. E. (1994). *Brain gym, teachers edition.* Ventura, CA: Edu-Kinesthetics.

Dewey, J. (1933). *How we think: A restatement of the relation of reflective thinking to the educative process.* Boston: Houghton Mifflin.

Diamond, M., & Hopson, J. (1998). *Magic trees of the mind: How to nurture your child's intelligence, creativity, and healthy emotions from birth through adolescence.* New York: Dutton-Penguin Putnam.

Dickmann, M. H., & Stanford-Blair, N. (2002). *Connecting leadership to the brain.* Thousand Oaks, CA: Corwin Press.

Drucker, P. F. (1973). *Management: Tasks, responsibilities, practices.* New York: Harper & Row.

Drucker, P. F. (1992). *Managing for the future: The 1990s and beyond.* New York: Penquin Books.

DuFour, R., & Eaker, R. (1998). *Professional learning communities at work: Best practices for enhancing student achievement.* Alexandria, VA: Association for Supervision and Curriculum Development

Ekman, P. (1984). Expression and nature of emotion. In K. Scherer and P. Ekman (Eds.), *Approaches to emotion* (pp. 319–343). Hillside, NJ: Erlbaum.

Eisner, E. (2002). *The arts and the creation of mind.* New Haven, CT: Yale University Press.

Fauconnier, G., & Turner, M. (2002). *The way we think: Conceptual blendings and the mind's hidden complexities.* New York: Basic Books.

Fogarty, R. (2002). *Brain compatible classrooms.* Arlington Heights, IL: Skylight Learning & Publishing.

Fullan, M. (1991). *The new meaning of educational change.* New York: Teacher's College Press.

Fullan, M. (2001). *Leading in a culture of change.* San Francisco: Jossey-Bass.

Fullan, M. (2003). *The moral imperative of school leadership.* Thousand Oaks, CA: Corwin Press.

Gaarder, J. (1996). *Sophie's world: A novel about the history of philosophy.* New York: Berkley.

Gage, F. H. (2003). Brain, repair yourself. *Scientific American, 289*(3), 46–53.

Gardner, H. (1995). *Leading minds: An anatomy of leadership.* New York: Basic Books.

Gardner, H. (1997a). *Extraordinary minds.* New York: Basic Books.

Gardner, H. (1997b). *Intelligence: Multiple perspectives.* San Diego, CA: Harcourt Brace.

Gazzaniga, M. (1998). *The mind's past.* Berkeley: University of California Press.

Gladwell, M. (2000). *The tipping point: How little things can make a big difference.* New York: Little, Brown.

Goldberg, E. (2001). *The executive brain: Frontal lobes and the civilized mind.* New York: Oxford University Press.

Goleman, D. (1995). *Emotional intelligence: Why it can matter more than IQ.* New York: Bantam.

Goleman, D. (1998). *Working with emotional intelligence.* New York: Bantam.

Goleman, D., Boyatzis, R. E., & McKee, A. (2002). *Primal leadership: Realizing the power of emotional intelligence.* Cambridge, MA: Harvard Business School Press.

Gopnik, A., Meltzoff, A. N., & Kuhl, P. K. (1999). *The scientist in the crib: Minds, brains, and how children learn.* New York: William Morrow.

Greenough, W. T., & Black, J. E. (1987). Experience and brain development. *Child Development, 58*(3), 539–555.

Greenough, W. T., & Black, J. E. (1992). Induction of brain structure by experience: Substrates for cognitive development. In M. R. Gunnar & C. A. Nelson (Eds.), *Minnesota symposia on child psychology: Vol. 24. Developmental behavioral neuroscience* (pp. 155–200). Hillsdale, NJ: Erlbaum.

Hannaford, C. (1995). *Smart moves: Why learning is not all in your head.* Arlington, VA: Great Ocean Publishers.

Hart, L. (1983). *Human brain and human learning.* Village of Oak Creek, AZ: Books for Educators.

Hebb, D. O. (1949). *The organization of behavior.* New York: John Wiley.

Hunter, M. (1992). *Mastery teaching.* El Segundo, CA: TIP.

Jackson, P. (1995). *Sacred hoops: Spiritual lessons of an hardwood warrior.* New York: Hyperion.

Johnson, D., & Johnson, F. (2002). *Joining together: Group theory and group skills.* Boston, MA: Allyn and Bacon.

Johnson, D. W., & Johnson R. T. (1999). *Learning together and alone: Cooperative, competitive, and individualistic learning.* Boston: Allyn and Bacon.

Johnson, D. W., & Johnson R. T. (1988). *Creative conflict.* Edina, MN: Interaction Book Company.

Joyce, B. R., & Showers, B. (1982). The coaching of teaching. *Educational Leadership, 40*(1), 4–16.

Kagan, S. (1992). *Cooperative learning structures.* San Clemente, CA: Kagan Cooperative.

Langer, E. J. (1997). *The power of mindful learning.* Reading, MA: Addison-Wesley.

LeDoux, J. (1996). *The emotional brain: The mysterious underpinnings of emotional life.* New York: Simon & Schuster.

Leider, R. J. (1997). *The power of purpose: Creating meaning in your life and work.* San Francisco: Berrett-Koehler.

Lewin, K. (1951). *Field theory in social science.* New York: Harper.

Lezotte, L. (1997). *Learning for all.* Okemos, MI: Effective School Products.

Mandela, N. (1995). *Long walk to freedom.* London, UK: Abacus.

Marzano, R. M. (2003). *What works in schools: Translating research into action.* Alexandria, VA: Association for Supervision and Curriculum Development.

Marzano, R. M. and Pickering, D. J. (1997). *Dimensions of learning Teacher's Manual.* Alexandria, VA: Association for Supervision and Curriculum Development.

Marzano, R. M., Norford, J. S., Paynter, D. E., Pickering, D. J., & Gaddy, B. B. (2001). *A handbook for classroom instruction that works.* Alexandria, VA: Association for Supervision and Curriculum Development.

Michalko, M. (1998). *Cracking creativity: The secrets of creative genius.* Berkeley, CA: Ten Speed Press.

Mintzberg, H. (1994). *The rise and fall of strategic planning.* New York: Free Press.

Mithen, S. (1996). *The prehistory of the mind: The cognitive origins of art, religion and science*. London: Thames & Hudson.

Northouse, P. G. (1997). *Leadership, theory and practice*. Thousand Oaks, CA: Sage.

Ogle, D. (1986). KWL: A teaching model that develops active reading of expository text. *The Reading Teacher, 39*, 564–576.

Owen, H. (1997). *Expanding our now: The story of open space technology*. San Francisco: Berrett-Koehler.

Parry, T., & Gregory, G. (1998). *Designing brain-compatible learning*. Arlington Heights, IL: Skylight Learning & Publishing.

Perkins, D. (1992). *Smart schools: From training memories to educating minds*. New York: Free Press.

Perkins, D. (1995). *Outsmarting IQ: The emerging science of learnable intelligence*. New York: Free Press.

Perkins, D. (2003).*King Arthur's round table: How collaborative conversations create smart organizations*. Hoboken, NJ: John Wiley.

Pert, C. B. (1997). *Molecules of emotion: Why you feel the way you feel*. New York: Scribner.

Peters, T. J., & Waterman, R. H. (1982). *In search of excellence*. New York: Harper and Row.

Pfeffer, J., & Sutton, R. I. (2002). *The knowing-doing gap: How smart companies turn knowledge into action*. Boston: Harvard Business School Press.

Pinker, S. (1997). *How the mind works*. New York: Norton.

Pinker, S. (2002). *The blank slate: The modern denial of human nature*. New York: Viking.

Restak, R. M. (2001). *The secret life of the brain*. Washington, DC: The Dana Press and the Joseph Henry Press.

Ridley, M. (1996). *The origins of virtue: Human instincts and the evolution of cooperation*. New York: Penguin.

Rost, J. C. (1991). *Leadership for the twenty-first century*. Westport, CT: Praeger.

Salovey, P., & Mayer, J. D. (1990). Emotional intelligence. *Imagination, Cognition, and Personality, 9*, 185–211.

Sapher, J., & King, M. (1985). Good seeds grow in strong cultures. *Educational leadership, March*, 15–20.

Sapolsky, R. (1994). *Why zebras don't get ulcers: An updated guide to stress, stress-related diseases, and coping*. New York: Freeman.

Schaie, K. W., & Willis, S. L. (1986). Can decline in adult intellectual functioning be reversed? *Developmental Psychology, 22*(2), 223.

Schein, E. (1991). *Organizational culture and leadership*. San Francisco: Jossey-Bass.

Schmoker, M. (1999). *Results: The key to continuous school improvement*. Alexandria, VA: Association for Supervision and Curriculum Development.

Schwartz, J. M., & Begley, S. (2002). *The mind and the brain: Neural plasticity and the power of mental force*. New York: HarperCollins.

Senge, P. M. (1990). *The fifth discipline: The art and practice of the learning organization*. New York: Doubleday.

Senge, P., Kleiner, A., Roberts, C., Ross, R., & Smith, B. (1994). *The fifth discipline fieldbook: Strategies and tools for building a learning organization*. New York: Doubleday Currency.

Sharan, S., & Sharan, Y. (1976). *Small-group teaching.* Englewood Cliffs, NJ: Educational Technology.

Siegel, D. (1999). *The developing mind: Toward a neurobiology of interpersonal experience.* New York: Guilford.

Simon, P. (1975). *50 ways to leave your lover.* Warner Bros. Records.

Slavin, R. E. (1990). *Cooperative learning: Theory, research, and practice.* Englewood Cliffs, NJ: Prentice Hall.

Snowdon, D. (2001). *Aging with grace: What the nun study teaches us about leading longer, healthier, and more meaningful lives.* New York: Bantam.

Sternberg, R. J. (1996). *Successful intelligence: How practical and creative intelligence determine success in life.* New York: Simon & Schuster.

Sylwester, R. (2000). *A biological brain in a cultural classroom: Applying biological research to classroom management.* Thousand Oaks, CA: Corwin Press.

Tishman, S. (2000). Why teach habits of mind? In A. L. Costa and B. Kallick (Eds.), *Discovering and exploring habits of mind.* Alexandria, VA: Association for Supervision and Curriculum Development.

van der Heijden, K. (1994). In P. Senge, A. Kleiner, C. Roberts, R. Ross, & B. Smith, *The fifth discipline fieldbook: Strategies and tools for building a learning organization.* New York: Doubleday Currency.

Vaughan, S. C. (2000). *Half empty, half full: Understanding the psychological roots of optimism.* San Diego, CA: Harcourt.

Vertosick, F. T. (2002). *The genius within: Discovering the intelligence of every living thing.* New York: Harcourt.

von Oech, R. (1990). *A whack on the side of the head: How you can be more creative.* Stamford, CT: U.S. Games Systems.

Vygotsky, L. (1978). *Mind in society: The development of higher psychological processes.* Cambridge, MA: Harvard University Press.

Weisbord, M. R., & Janoff, S. (1995) *Future search: An action guide to finding common ground in organizations and communities.* San Francisco: Berrett-Koehler.

Welch, J. (2001). *Jack: Straight from the gut.* New York: Warner Books.

Wheatley, M. J. (1992). *Leadership and the new science: Learning about organization from an orderly universe.* San Francisco: Berrett-Koehler.

Wheatley, M. J. (2002). *Turning to one another: Simple conversations to restore hope to the future.* San Francisco: Berrett-Koehler.

Index

**CORWIN
PRESS**

The Corwin Press logo—a raven striding across an open book—represents the union of courage and learning. Corwin Press is committed to improving education for all learners by publishing books and other professional development resources for those serving the field of K–12 education. By providing practical, hands-on materials, Corwin Press continues to carry out the promise of its motto: "**Helping Educators Do Their Work Better**."